Wake up and Live!

Wake up and Live!

An abridgement of Joseph Alleine's Alarm to the Unconverted' rewritten in modern English. The full version is available from The Banner of Truth Trust, 3 Murrayfield Road, Edinburgh EH12 6EL

**Prepared by
Norman Wells**

GRACE PUBLICATIONS TRUST
139 Grosvenor Avenue
London N5 2NH
England

Joint Managing Editors:

J. P. Arthur M. A.
H. J. Appleby

ISBN 0 946462 50X

Distributed by:

Evangelical Press
Faverdale North Industrial Estate
Darlington
DL3 0PH

Bible quotations, unless otherwise indicated, are taken from
the Revised Authorized Version

Cover design and artwork by L. L. Evans

Printed in Great Britain by: Creative Print and Design
(Wales), Ebbw Vale

Contents

Introduction

I have written this book for people who are not yet Christians. My hope and prayer is that through reading it you will turn to God. But I am very conscious of the fact that no matter how hard I try and no matter how persuasive my arguments are, by myself I cannot make anyone become a Christian. That is something only God can do.

The Bible says that you must be born again to go to heaven. Without holiness you will never see God (Hebrews 12:14). As you begin to read, make up your mind to seek God. Be prepared to acknowledge Jesus Christ as Lord with all your heart. Submit to him and you will live!

You may find some of the things I say hard to take. I certainly don't expect to make myself popular — but then that is not my aim! For myself, I would much rather write a more enjoyable book, but if you are not a Christian, your position is much too serious for that. It's all very well to sing a crying baby to sleep, but something more drastic is required if a young child has fallen into the fire.

A good doctor will always show the most concern for the patient whose life is in the greatest danger. And a good father will always give special attention to his dying child. The greater the need, the greater the compassion and effort that are required.

I shall therefore try to write very plainly about your greatest need. I am not ashamed to say that I hope you will not only be convinced by what I write, but also converted to Jesus Christ and saved.

Some of you may be unsure as to what a Christian is. I shall therefore begin by addressing the question, **What is a Christian?**

Others may imagine that all is well between them and God when in fact it is not. For them I will explain about **becoming a Christian.**

Then there will be those who wonder whether it is important for them to become Christians. I shall therefore deal with the question, **Does it really matter?**

Others may claim to be Christians when they give no real evidence of this in the way they live. To them I will attempt to show **the way we are** before we turn to Christ.

Others *fear* no danger because they don't *feel* any. I must therefore show that without Christ we are all **condemned!**

Then there are some who are aware of their need but don't know what to do about it. I shall therefore answer their question, **What must I do?**

And finally, for the benefit of all, I shall point you to the **amazing grace** of God.

Joseph Alleine 1671

1.
What is a Christian?

The question needs to be raised because it is being answered in all kinds of different ways. The result is that some people imagine they are Christians when they aren't, and others think they are not Christians when they really are! In the next chapter I shall explain what it means to become a Christian, but first of all, let me tell you what it doesn't mean.

1. It's not enough just to call yourself a Christian

Christianity is much more than a name. The Bible talks about some people who claimed to be Christians and belonged to a church without being true Christians at all. Sadly there are many people who profess to be followers of the Lord Jesus Christ, but who show by the way they live that they have never really turned away from their sins. They may claim to know God, but their lives deny it. In fact, the Lord Jesus warned that it is possible even to preach and perform miracles in his name without being a real Christian (Titus 1:16; Matthew 7:22-23). After all, how can people say God has saved them from their sins when they haven't given them up?

2. It's not enough to be baptized

It is quite a common idea to think that baptism makes you a Christian. Many people think that because they have gone through a form of baptism they are children of God and sure to go to heaven. But if baptism really made you a Christian and earned you God's favour, all you would need to go to heaven would be a certificate of baptism! Millions of people have been baptised, but the Lord Jesus Christ says 'narrow is the gate and difficult is the way that leads to life, and there are few who find it' (Matthew 7:13-14). He also speaks of seeking, knocking and wrestling to enter heaven (Matthew 11:12; Luke 13:24). All this would be quite unnecessary if baptism were all that were needed. Baptism is a sign of what God has done for us. In itself it does nothing. Baptism is good, but it is no substitute for the thorough and powerful change that Jesus called being 'born again' (John 3:7).

3. It's not enough to live a good clean life

In Bible times, there was no group of people more particular about good clean living than the Jewish scribes and Pharisees. But the Lord Jesus Christ declared, 'Unless your righteousness exceeds the righteousness of the scribes and Pharisees, you will by no means enter the kingdom of heaven' (Matthew 5:20). You don't have to be a Christian to live a good clean life. Long before he became a Christian, the apostle Paul could claim that he was blameless in his lifestyle (Philippians 3:6). But it wasn't enough. You need more than this or else God will still condemn you, no matter how much you protest your innocence. I am not against morality; I simply warn you not to rely on it. Good clean living never saved anyone.

4. It's not enough to be religious

The Bible says it is possible to have a form of religion without any reality or spiritual power (2 Timothy 3:5). You can pray long prayers, listen to religious preaching and teaching, fast, and do all kinds of other things to serve God without being a real Christian (Matthew 23:14; Luke 18:12; Mark 6:20;

Isaiah 1:11). True Christianity involves much more than going to church, being generous with your money and saying your prayers. You can do all these things - and even lay down your life - and yet still not really belong to God.

5. It's not enough to reform yourself

The Bible teaches that it is quite possible for you to have your mind enlightened with regard to the things of God and to feel guilty about your sins, and yet still to fall short of becoming a Christian (Hebrews 6:4; Acts 24:25; Mark 6:20). There is a distinct difference between conviction and conversion. Cain, the first man ever to commit a murder, restlessly wandered from place to place with his troubled conscience until he managed to stifle it with business and building projects. But there is nothing in the Bible to suggest that he ever really sought God (Genesis 4). Some people imagine they are Christians simply because they have stopped committing a particular sin, given up a bad habit or distanced themselves from certain evil influences. But there is far more to becoming a Christian than any of these things.

While their consciences are troubled, many people will pray, read the Bible, listen to preaching and give up some of their sinful pleasures, but as soon as they don't feel convicted any longer, they go straight back to their sins. There was never a more religious group of people than the Jews when God's hand was against them, but when their period of suffering was over, they invariably forgot God again. You may have reformed your life in any number of ways and yet still be exactly the same person at heart.

You can take a lump of clay and mould it into a flower, then into an animal, then into the shape of a man, but all the time

11

it remains clay. In the same way, any one of us can move from ignorance to knowledge and from open ungodliness to a form of religion while our nature is the same as it always was.

If you have been basing your hopes on some of the things we have discussed so far, you may have found this chapter difficult to accept. It can be a painful experience to realise that all is not well between you and God when you might have thought that it was. As I have been writing I have felt a little like a surgeon about to amputate the limb of a close friend - not for pleasure but out of necessity. It is far better for you to realise the situation you are in now, rather than continue with your false hopes and end up in hell.

If you claim to be a Christian, let me invite you to examine the basis of your hope:

Is it because you have been baptized?
Is it because you are a church member?
Is it because you know quite a lot about religion?
Is it because you try to live a good clean moral life?
Is it because you have felt troubled by your sins?

All these things are very good in themselves, but they do not make you a Christian, and they will not save you. Examine yourself and turn to the Lord with all your heart. Unless God himself changes you, you will be lost.

But perhaps you do not claim to be a Christian at all. If so, your position is certainly no better. You too must repent of your sins and be converted. Turn to the Lord Jesus Christ. Receive his forgiveness and new life. Give yourself over to him and live a holy life, or else you will never see God. If you stay as you are, you will suffer eternal death for sure.

2.
Becoming a Christian

Now that we have looked at several of the most common misconceptions some people have about what a Christian is, it is time to think about what it *really* means to become a Christian.

1. The Holy Spirit must change you

The Bible describes becoming a Christian as a 'sanctification by the Spirit' (2 Thessalonians 2:13) and 'the renewing of the Holy Spirit' (Titus 3:5). While God the Father and the Lord Jesus Christ are also most certainly involved (see for example 1 Peter 1:3; Acts 5:31), the Bible shows that it is principally the work of the Holy Spirit to make people Christians. The Lord Jesus therefore describes a Christian as someone who has been 'born of the Spirit' (John 3:5-6).

In other words, becoming a Christian is beyond our human power and ability. The Bible says that a Christian is 'born, not of blood, nor of the will of the flesh, nor of the will of man, but of God' (John 1:13). You can never make yourself a child of God and nobody else can make you one either. Becoming a Christian is described in terms of a resurrection from the dead (Ephesians 2:1) and only God can do that. The Bible also likens it to being made a new creation (2 Corinthians 5:17). Again, only God can create and make things new. Men and women can form, mould and fashion, but God alone is the Creator.

2. You need God's grace

God is under no obligation to do anything for any one of us. No one 'deserves' his favour. The Bible says that God saves us, 'not by works of righteousness which we have done, but *according to his mercy*' (Titus 3:5). It is '*of his own will* [that he brings] us forth by the word of truth' (James 1:18), and the apostle Paul makes it clear that God the Father chooses and calls people *to* holiness and not *for* any measure of holiness to which they have already attained (Ephesians 1:4). No one ever does, nor ever can do, anything to earn or deserve the powerful work of the Holy Spirit.

God finds nothing at all in us to turn his heart towards us. Rather, there is plenty to turn him away and provoke his holy anger. By nature we are sinful, wicked, rebellious, deceitful, disobedient and ungodly, while God is holy, pure, sinless, righteous, just, true and good. It is entirely due to his grace that such a God loves us at all. By *grace*, I mean that the Lord shows patience and kindness to us even though we deserve quite the opposite. You would think that people would be for ever praising God and telling others about his grace! And yet many of us are so ungrateful that we hardly ever stop to think about God's grace and when we do, it is often only in a very cold and formal way. By contrast the apostle Peter exclaims, 'Blessed be the God and Father of our Lord Jesus Christ, who according to his abundant mercy has begotten us again to a living hope' (1 Peter 1:3)! Paul writes with similar feeling, 'But God, who is rich in mercy, because of his great love with which he has loved us, even when we were dead in trespasses, made us alive together with Christ (by grace you have been saved)' (Ephesians 2:4-5).

3. Jesus Christ has done it all

Without the Lord Jesus Christ, no one would be able to come to God. The Bible says, 'There is one God and one mediator between God and men, the man Christ Jesus' (1 Timothy 2:5). If it were not for Jesus becoming man, obeying God's law, dying on the cross and rising again, we could never be reconciled to God. He is the only way, the only hope.

Through the work of the Lord Jesus Christ, God gives every spiritual blessing in the heavenly places to his people (Ephesians 1:3). While still here on earth, Jesus specifically prayed for those who would later believe in him (John 17:20), and everyone who becomes a Christian does so as a result of his suffering and death on the cross (Hebrews 10:10). The sufferings and prayers of Christ are the only basis on which God changes any of us and makes us Christians. If you are a new creature, a true Christian, you owe it all to Christ. To whom else can you go? Can anyone show a greater love than him? Your own sinful inclinations, the world around you and the devil himself may all try to win your heart, but none of them was ever crucified for you as Christ was. The Lord Jesus stands alone as being worthy of your love and service.

4. God uses the Bible to bring you to himself

The Bible is the means God uses to draw men, women and children to himself. Only the Bible can give us light and understanding and convert our souls (Psalm 19:7-8). The apostle Paul writes that the Bible makes us wise for salvation (2 Timothy 3:15), and Peter says it is the incorruptible seed by which we are born again (1 Peter 1:23). The Bible, the Word of God, brings us to faith in Christ and gives us new life (Romans 10:17; James 1:18). The psalmist exclaims, 'I will never forget your precepts; for by them you have given me life' (Psalm 119:93). Christians have every reason to be thankful for the Bible and to treasure it!

If you are seeking God, it is important to read the Bible very thoughtfully and carefully. If at all possible, try to find a church where you can hear it faithfully preached. God has called preachers to open the eyes of their hearers and turn them back to himself (Acts 26:18). He has appointed and equipped them to show you the way of salvation (Acts 16:17). Resist the temptation to criticise them and insult them, but rather listen to them and pray that God will help you to understand the message they preach.

5. Every part of you will be affected

As we have seen, only God can make you a Christian. The Lord Jesus says that no one can come to him unless God the Father draws him. But at the same time he promises that he will never turn away anyone who comes to him (John 6:37,44). We cannot begin to understand how these two truths tie up, and thankfully we don't need to understand it because God's promises and commands are very clear. The Bible says, 'Repent and be converted that your sins may be blotted out' (Acts 3:19). 'Believe on the Lord Jesus Christ and you will be saved' (Acts 16:31). If I repent and believe, I can be sure I shall be saved. But if I do not repent, I shall be condemned. Nothing could be plainer than that!

We come now to consider in greater detail the radical change that takes place when you become a Christian. It's not like repairing an old building but more like putting up a new one. It's not a matter of sewing on a patch of holiness but rather of having holiness woven into every area of your life. A true

16

Christian is a new creature: all things have become new (2 Corinthians 5:17).

(a) You will think differently

When you become a Christian, you will begin to see things from a different perspective. In the past you may have seen no danger in your condition, but now God has opened your eyes and you can appreciate the seriousness of your plight without him. You may have seen no harm in sin, but now you see sin for the great evil that it is and you begin to hate it, dread it and run from it. You will find that you even hate yourself because of it. As the Lord said to Ezekiel, 'You will remember your evil ways and your deeds that were not good; and you will loathe yourselves in your own sight, for your iniquities and your abominations' (Ezekiel 36:31). Previously you may not have thought there was very much wrong with you at all and you may have seen no real need to confess your sins to God. However, now you are only too painfully aware of the fact that you are unclean and corrupt in God's sight. All that you are and everything you do is tainted by sin. You will begin to see sins in your life that you didn't know were there before - even ugly sins like blasphemy, theft, murder and adultery in your heart. Up until now you may not have felt any attraction towards the Lord Jesus Christ, but now he is more precious to you than anything in all the world.

When you start thinking in this new way, everything else will fade into insignificance compared with knowing that God is pleased with you. Of course, anyone can *say* in a general kind of way that God is the most important Person of all, but when you become a Christian, God *really does* become the most important Person to you. That is the big difference. From your heart you will be able to pray:

17

Whom have I in heaven but you?
And there is none upon earth that I desire besides you.
My flesh and my heart fail;
But God is the strength of my heart and my
portion for ever (Psalm 73:25-26)

(b) You will have new priorities

As a Christian you will have new goals and a new purpose. Your biggest aim of all will be to honour Christ and to serve him. This will bring you more joy and happiness than anything else in the whole world. There is nothing more worthwhile than making the name of Jesus more widely known and loved.

When you become a Christian you start making decisions that you could never possibly have made before. You see in God everything you could ever want and you entrust yourself to Jesus Christ to bring you to him. You are not *forced* to come to Christ by any personal difficulties you may be having at the time, but you positively *choose* to come to him. And that choice isn't made in a moment of panic because your conscience is troubled and you are afraid of going to hell. No! You are absolutely convinced that Christ is the best choice of all and you would rather have him than all the good things the world has to offer. The same goes for living a holy life. You don't choose to obey God because you feel you *have* to, but because you *want* to. You love God's ways and you want to obey him. Far from being a burden to you, God's commandments become your joy and delight (1 John 5:3; Psalm 119:14,16,47)!

When people are ill, they sometimes strongly dislike the taste of their medicine. The only reason they take it is because their lives depend on it. But the Christian life isn't like that at all.

18

Christians don't follow Christ because they *have* to, but because they *want* to. God's commandments are nothing like a dreaded medicine. They are more like food to someone who is desperately hungry. There is nothing more satisfying!

(c) You will have a different outlook on life

You will be willing to part with anything and everything so long as you can keep Christ. You would rather be like him than be rich and famous. As a non-Christian you may have dreamed about being universally admired and financially secure without a care in the world. But when you become a Christian, all that changes. Now you say to yourself, 'If only I were not so sinful! If only I could be closer to God! Even if I didn't have much money and other people hated me, I would still be happy!' Can you say that?

As a Christian, you will find your happiness in different things. At one time the Bible may have seemed very dull and even boring to you, but now there is nothing that gives you greater pleasure. There is nothing to compare with the joy of thinking about Christ, with enjoying his company and with seeing his people prosper. No longer will you be completely preoccupied with things you can see, hear, touch and taste; the salvation of your soul will now be your greatest concern.

From now on, you will be more afraid of sinning than of suffering. Perhaps you used to worry about losing your property or your reputation and you shuddered at the thought of pain, poverty and disgrace. But now all these concerns fade into insignificance compared with your fear of dishonouring God. You are constantly on guard against traps that could lead you into sin. Nothing causes you greater pain than the thought of drifting away from Christ.

19

Along with a strong love for Christ, it is only fair to add that you will also have new sorrows and sadnesses. The thought of your sins and of Christ on the cross may not have moved you before, but now they fill you with grief. Your anger will burn against sin - your own sins as much as anyone else's. There will be times when you struggle to find an appropriate word to express how badly you feel about yourself. In the past you could wallow in sin and find pleasure in it, but now you hate the thought of returning to a life of sin as much as the thought of wallowing in the filthiest muck.

Take time now to think carefully about whether your feelings are directed more towards God and Christ than anything else. It is quite possible for you to feel some degree of devotion to the Lord Jesus without being a real Christian - especially if you are a warm person by nature. On the other hand, it is equally possible to be a Christian without feeling these emotions to any great extent if your temperament is more cool and placid. But the crucial question is whether you put God first in your thinking and decision-making. If you do, then that is a good sign that the Lord has saved you, even if your feelings are not as strong as you may wish.

(d) Your body will belong to God

When you turn to Christ, your body becomes the temple of the Holy Sprit. You dedicate your eyes, ears, head, heart and mouth to God. One could almost say that becoming a Christian affects every part of your body!

Your eyes, which were once so proud, so covetous, so restless, will now weep over your sins, admire God's wonderful work in creation, read his Word the Bible and constantly look out for opportunities to serve him and help people in need.

20

Your ears, which were once open to the devil and enjoyed nothing more than listening to the latest gossip and ungodly jokes, will now be wide open to the words of Christ and his followers. The words of God will be far more precious to you than the idle words of men. Like Samuel, you will say to God, 'Speak, Lord, for your servant hears.' You will consider God's words of greater value than even your daily food (Job 23:12; Psalm 19:10).

Your head, which was once full of ambitious plans to increase your wealth and comfort, will now be filled with thoughts of how you can please God and avoid sin.

Your heart, which was once so full of impure desires, will now be inspired by love for God and will overflow in prayer and praise.

You will no longer use **your mouth** to flatter, boast, insult, lie, swear and engage in unwholesome talk. Instead, you will use your tongue to pray to the Lord and to speak in a way that is helpful to other people. You will never be happier than when you are speaking about God and the Lord Jesus Christ. And when you are talking about spiritual things it won't be to impress other people; your heart will be in it.

From time to time you will hear people insist, 'It's *my* life; I'll live how I like!' But that's not the language of a Christian. The believer says, 'It's *not* my life. My life belongs to the God who gave it to me. He created me and he has redeemed me. My body is a temple of the Holy Spirit. I belong to the Lord and I live, not to please myself, but to serve him.'

6. You will put the past behind you

The difference between a Christian and a non-Christian is as great as the difference between life and death. In Ephesians 2:1-3, the apostle Paul expresses the contrast in a particularly vivid way. Writing to people who had recently become Christians, he declares: 'And you [God] made alive, who were dead in trespasses and sins, in which you once walked, according to the course of this world, according to the prince of the power of the air, the spirit who now works in the sons of disobedience, among whom also we all once conducted ourselves in the lusts of our flesh, fulfilling the desires of the flesh and of the mind, and were by nature children of wrath, just as the others.' When Almighty God produces this tremendous change in you, you become a citizen of heaven itself (Philippians 3:20). The Lord gives you a new heart and writes his law in your mind so that you want to please him in everything.

This is not, of course, to say that you will immediately become perfect. Sin will continue to live within you, though now as an unwelcome guest rather than as your master. But even though you will continue to sin, your overriding concern will be to honour and obey the Lord Jesus in matters both large and small. If you really belong to Christ, you won't be one person at church and another at home. You won't be a saint on your knees but a cheat at work. You won't make a big fuss about minor religious practices while neglecting the larger and all-embracing parts of God's law. And you won't pretend to be religious and yet refuse to allow your religion to affect every part of your life. Rather you will turn from all your sins and aim to keep all God's commandments. You will find pleasure in reading the Bible, in praying to God and in showing a genuine concern for those in need.

So many people who consider themselves good Christians are in the habit of picking and choosing which commandments they will keep and which they will ignore. They tend to adopt a form of religion which is easy to observe and which costs them little. For example, you may find them very precise in the words they use and committed to helping others, but they have less interest in seriously examining themselves and pursuing holiness in their hearts. They may be regular churchgoers, but in their homes they are often no different from people who make no Christian profession at all. They may even spend time in private or family prayer, yet at work they make no effort to control their tongues. James writes, 'If anyone among you thinks he is religious and does not bridle his tongue but deceives his own heart, this one's religion is useless' (James 1:26). A false Christian is not thorough in his obedience. But when you become a true Christian, you turn your back on everything to do with sin, Satan, the world and your own righteousness.

(a) You will turn from sin

When you put your trust in Christ, sin becomes an enemy to you - especially your own sins. You learn to hate sin and to recognise it as the root of all your problems. Like the apostle Paul, you will groan and struggle under it and long to be free from its destructive influence. In your days as a non-Christian, perhaps you did not take sin particularly seriously. You may have loved it and enjoyed indulging in it, but as soon as God opens your eyes, you begin to see it in a different light. You see its danger and its filthiness and you long to be made clean. You come to hate yourself for your sins and you hurry to Christ and ask him to purify you. Then if, as a Christian, you fall into some sin, you instinctively want to be made clean again.

Every true Christian is engaged in a battle against sin. He struggles with it, he wars against it and, although he is all too often foiled by it, he never gives in. He constantly perseveres. While we can forgive our other enemies and pray for them, we can never do that with sin. We can never make peace with it. Nothing less than its complete extermination will do. Sin can never be tolerated, not even if it 'pays' in worldly terms. A Christian would rather lose popularity and wealth, and miss out on legitimate pleasures than give way to sin.

Has your conscience been at work while you have been reading these lines? Are you battling against sin? Have you turned away from your sins? If not, then it is clear that you are not yet a Christian and unless God changes you, you will be condemned.

(b) You will turn from Satan

A Christian believer is someone whom God has 'delivered from the power of darkness and translated into the kingdom of the Son of his love' (Colossians 1:13). Until then, the devil holds us as his captives. No sooner does Satan call us to get involved in bad company or engage in sinful pleasures than we are there ready and willing to do whatever he wants us to do. If he tempts us to lie, the words are right there on our tongues. If he encourages us to neglect our family responsibilities, we will do so. If he suggests that we are taking the Bible too seriously, we will readily agree with him. Or if he tells us that there is no real need for private prayer, again we will gladly remove it from our list of priorities.

All this changes when you become a Christian. You acknowledge the Lord Jesus Christ as your new Master and set yourself to serve him. While Satan may occasionally still

24

trap you and lure you into sin, you are no longer a willing captive. Rather you are constantly on your guard against his snares and baits and you make a point of acquainting yourself with his subtle methods. All the time you are careful to take steps to ensure that your great enemy will not be able to catch you off guard and take advantage of you.

(c) You will turn from the world

For the non-Christian this world is everything. All your hopes, all your dreams and all your ambitions are centred here. Whether you make an idol of money, pleasure or your own reputation, you are overcome by what the world has to offer and you have put something else in the place that rightly belongs to God alone.

What a terrible thing sin is! God made you 'a little lower than the angels,' but sin has made you little better than the devils. Sin has turned you into a kind of deformed monster which has its head and heart where its feet should be. Your feet kick against heaven and everything is out of place. The world that God created to serve you has risen up to rule you and dominate your life. But when the Lord has mercy on you, everything is put back in the right order. God is on the throne, Christ is in your heart and the world is under your feet, where it belongs. With the apostle Paul you can declare, 'the world has been crucified to me and I to the world' (Galatians 6:14). While the non-Christian is for ever seeking some new pleasure or source of satisfaction from the world, the Christian can address God and say, 'Whom have I in heaven but you? And there is none upon earth that I desire besides you. My flesh and my heart fail; but God is the strength of my heart and my portion for ever' (Psalm 73:25-26).

25

Nothing else and no one else can give lasting satisfaction. Every pleasure and enjoyment that the world can offer will ultimately leave you empty and frustrated. Without God, 'all is vanity' (Ecclesiastes 1:2), but with God life takes on new meaning and purpose. When you become a Christian, your heart is set on seeking God and his kingdom and righteousness. Religion is no longer a matter of indifference to you, but your chief interest and concern. Godliness becomes more important than gain. No longer must God stand by waiting until you have finished serving the world. Everything else now takes second place to Christ.

Examine yourself. Perhaps you pretend to be on the side of Christ, but all the time you are swayed by worldly considerations - by money, pleasure, fame or popularity. Do you take more delight in the world than in Jesus, the Son of God? Are you more at home thinking about things you can see and taste and touch than when you are worshipping God and meditating on his Word? If the things of the world are uppermost in your mind and take up most of your emotional energy, it is a sign that you are not right with God.

For the true Christian, the Lord Jesus Christ is supreme. His name is dear and his favour is precious. Everything else fades into the background when you trust the Saviour. He is your treasure, he is your hope, he is your life! It is far, far better to be able to say 'Christ is mine' than it would be to say 'The whole world is mine.'

(d) You will turn from your own righteousness

Before people become Christians they are inclined to imagine that they can make themselves acceptable to God by their own efforts. But when the Lord opens your eyes and shows

26

you what you are really like, you begin to see your imagined righteousness for what it really is - filthy rags. You want to throw it away, just as you would the infested clothes of a scruffy beggar. You are humbled before the Holy One and recognise that there is nothing pure about even your religious practices. The goodness you once admired in yourself, you now acknowledge to be worthless filth.

The righteousness of Christ is the only righteousness that really counts with God. And the more you see your own lack of righteousness, the more you see your need of Christ's righteousness. You need Christ for everything. You need him to be able to stand before God and you need him to change you inwardly. You can neither pray nor even live without him. Without Christ you can never enter the presence of the Lord. Only the perfect and spotless Saviour can usher you into the throne-room of the infinitely holy God. You cannot hope to approach him on your own. When you begin to appreciate these truths, the Christian gospel is no longer a stale and tasteless thing to you; it is rather the most wonderful message of all! The true Christian takes no credit for the spiritual change he has experienced. He gladly acknowledges that he is indebted to Christ and to Christ alone.

7. You will turn to God with all your heart

When you become a Christian, there is nothing and no one more precious to you than the one true God. He is everything to you. You will be able to say with the Psalmist, 'In God is my salvation and my glory; the rock of my strength and my refuge is in God' (Psalm 62:7).

What makes you really happy? What do you long for more than anything else? If the Lord were to say to you, 'Ask me

27

for whatever you wish and you may have it,' what would you ask for? Would endless pleasure satisfy you? Or great wealth? Or popularity? Would any one of these things - or all of them put together - make you happy? If you think they would, it is a clear sign that you have never turned to God with all your heart. But if you recognise that there is nothing on earth that can satisfy the deepest needs and longings of your soul, I encourage you to explore the perfect character of God. His mercy is overflowing. His mighty power will surround you on all sides. There is no limit to his resources. You will find him sufficient for all your needs. What more could you want? If the Lord can make you happy, you will be happy indeed because you have taken him to be your God. If all is well between you and God, you have every reason to be happy. Like the apostle Peter you will want to say to the Lord Jesus, 'Lord, to whom shall I go? You have the words of eternal life' (John 6:68). There is no longer any need to run here and there in an endless pursuit of peace and joy. When you turn to God, your days of restlessness are over and you can say to yourself, 'Return to your rest O my soul, for the Lord has dealt bountifully with you' (Psalm 116:7).

In particular, when you become a Christian you turn to Christ, the only Mediator between God and the human race (1 Timothy 2:5). He is the way to the Father (John 14:6), the only door into his presence (John 10:9). The very reason he died on the cross was to bring us to God (1 Peter 3:18). There is no one else who can save us and give us new life. Conscious of your sin, you flee to him in desperation: 'I will come to Christ and if I perish, I perish; if I die, I will die here. But Lord, do not let me perish under the eye of your mercy. Do not allow me to leave you or to give up following you. I want to be with you for ever.'

Previously, you may not have taken the Lord Jesus all that seriously. Your career, your friends and your possessions may have meant much more to you than Christ. But now he is your life. Nothing is worth comparing with him. Everything about him is worthy of love and praise and, in addition to enjoying his blessings, you find yourself willing to serve him and even to suffer for him.

Sadly, you may come across people who only want half a Saviour. They say they want to be saved by Christ, but they aren't interested in having their lives changed by him. They are interested in all the good gifts he gives to his people, but they don't appreciate Christ himself. In effect, they are trying to separate what Jesus does from who he is. The Bible tells us that God raised Jesus from the dead and exalted him to be 'Prince and Saviour' (Acts 5:31) - the King who takes control of our lives, as well as the Priest who offered himself to take away our sins. We must never try to divide what God has joined. Everyone wants to be saved from suffering but not everyone wants to be saved from sinning. You must be very careful at this point. A real Christian trusts Christ as he is, without reservation. He is willing to have him as Lord as well as Saviour. Like the apostle Paul, in a spirit of submission he cries out, 'Lord, what would you have me to do?' (Acts 9:6).

In turning to Christ, we also turn to his laws and ways. At one time, God's commandments will have appeared unattractive, strict and severe to you, but when he changes your heart, you fall in love with them and freely choose them as your rule and guide for ever. There will be no doubt in your mind that God's commandments are 'holy, just and good' (Romans 7:12) and, along with David, you will be able to testify:

The law of the Lord is perfect, converting the soul;
The testimony of the Lord is sure, making wise the
    simple;
The statutes of the Lord are right, rejoicing the heart;
The commandment of the Lord is pure, enlightening
    the eyes;
The fear of the Lord is clean, enduring for ever;
The judgements of the Lord are true and righteous
    altogether.
More to be desired are they than gold, yea, than much
    fine gold;
Sweeter also than honey and the honeycomb
    (Psalm 19:7-10).

Some people think that God's commandments are appropriate for most people, but somehow they find a way of excusing themselves. They try to convince themselves that they are exempt; their circumstances are exceptional. But if you are a true Christian, you will view the commandments of God not merely as best in general terms, but as best for *you*. They are not merely tolerable, but desirable. Psalm 119 perfectly expresses the judgement of a godly person:

I love your commandments more than gold, yes than
    fine gold!
Therefore all your precepts concerning all things I
    consider to be right;
I hate every false way...
Righteous are you, O Lord, and upright are your
    judgements.
Your testimonies which you have commanded are
    righteous and very faithful...
Your righteousness is an everlasting righteousness,
    and your law is truth.
        (Psalm 119:127, 128, 137, 138, 142, 144).

Such a commitment to do the will of God means that you will be concerned to detect any sins or shortcomings in your life. You will no longer be content to cover up your sins or to remain ignorant of them. It will be natural for you to pray, 'Lord, show me if there is any sin in my heart. And please teach me what you require of me. If I have sinned against you, I will turn from that sin.'

You will not only be keen to have your sins exposed, but you will also want to know what God wants you to do so that you can please and honour him. There is no sense of wearisome obligation or of panic as you seek to do God's will, but rather an enthusiasm to follow the Lord Jesus Christ. When the Lord touches your heart you will find that his commandments bring you freedom and you begin to serve him not slavishly, but willingly, out of a spirit of love. Although you will continue to fall short of God's standards, your aim will be for nothing less than perfection. You will have the same attitude as the apostle Paul in Philippians 3:12-14: 'I press on, that I may lay hold of that for which Christ Jesus has also laid hold of me...forgetting those things that are behind and reaching forward to those things that are ahead, I press towards the goal for the prize of the upward call of God in Christ Jesus.'

There is all the difference in the world between a true Christian who wants to be like Christ and the person who is interested in no more than a place in heaven. Some people want holiness merely as a bridge to heaven - the minimum will do; they don't want any more holiness than is absolutely necessary to save them from hell. But a true Christian wants holiness for its own sake and not merely for heaven's sake. How is it with you? Has Jesus Christ changed your whole way of life? Is holiness your number one goal?

I urge you once again to examine yourself. What does your conscience say to you? Does it accuse you? Does your heart condemn you and tell you of a certain sin you are living in? Does it tell you of other sins you would readily engage in given the slightest opportunity? Does it tell you that you owe certain duties to God that you have pushed to one side? Perhaps your conscience reminds you of your prayerlessness, your neglect of your children and your misuse of the time your kind Creator has given you. May your conscience be active and give you no rest until you have turned from your sins and returned to God with all your heart!

3.
Does it really matter?

Perhaps you are wondering, 'What's all the fuss about? Why does this man keep telling me I must repent and turn to Christ? Why doesn't he leave me alone?'

Let me assure you that if you could be saved as you are, I would gladly leave you alone. But the truth is that I can have no hope of seeing you in heaven unless you become a Christian. Unless you turn to God with all your heart and begin to live a new life, there is no way you can be saved. The Lord Jesus Christ has very plainly stated, 'Unless one is born again, he cannot see the kingdom of God' (John 3:3). This is not something that only very advanced Christians need to be concerned with; it is something that *everyone* needs in order to be saved.

A leading football manager in England once said, 'Football is not a matter of life and death; it's more important than that!' I wonder, what is vitally important to you? Your food? Your health? Your sporting interests? Let me tell you that becoming a Christian is even more vitally important. In fact it is the only thing that really matters. You can part with your possessions, your reputation and even lay down your life for Christ and have no regrets. But Christ himself is far more important.
You can't be saved without him.

Let me give you four reasons why you need to become a Christian:

1. Without Christ your life is meaningless

God made you for himself, but if you have never really turned to him, you cannot fulfil the purpose for which you were made. God has given you a mind and the ability to reason - you are 'fearfully and wonderfully made' (Psalm 139:14). Do you really think that the Lord created you just to please yourself and satisfy your own desires? Did he make people, like the swallows, just to gather a few sticks and mud, build their nests, rear their young and then fly away? Surely not!

Without God, your life has no meaning and purpose at all. And if you continue to live without him, it would have been better if you had never been born. In order to fulfil the purpose for which the Lord made you, you must repent and become a Christian. Without Christ, you are like a fine musical instrument which is out of tune or has broken strings. You need to be repaired and tuned by the work of the Holy Spirit or else none of your prayers and religious practices will ever please God.

Left to yourself, you are so sinful that you cannot serve the living God any more than you could hope to read without learning the alphabet. The Bible says that before you turn to Christ, you are utterly without strength to please God (Romans 5:6); you are dead in your sins (Ephesians 2:5). Indeed, you are not particularly interested in following God's ways. You might as well try painting without paint and brushs, or build a house without materials as try to serve God without the Holy Spirit. If you do not have a true love for the Lord in your heart, all your charitable giving, all your prayers and all your worship will be vain and empty. When the tree is bad, how can the fruit be good?

34

The Lord Jesus didn't mince his words when he spoke about the corruption of the human heart. He said, 'Out of the heart proceed evil thoughts, murders, adulteries, fornications, thefts, false witness, blasphemies' (Matthew 15:19). All this from the hearts of creatures made in the image of God! What a terrible thing to see the crown of God's creation in such a dreadful condition!

2. Without Christ your religion is meaningless

No matter what your religion may be and no matter how devout you are in it, you can never please God or save your soul without Christ (Romans 8:8). Even the most grand and impressive religious ceremonies are abominations to God and leave him unmoved (Isaiah 1:14; Proverbs 28:9; Malachi 1:10).

Many people, when they begin to feel the weight of their sins, imagine that a few prayers or a few generous gifts to those in need will put everything right, but what they really need is a thorough change of heart. Long before he became a Christian, the apostle Paul was *blameless* when it came to outwardly keeping God's law, but it didn't bring him God's favour (Philippians 3:6-7). Some people even think that they have done so much for the Lord that he *owes* them salvation. Nothing could be further from the truth! During those times when you become very conscious of your sins, never imagine that a little praying and self-reformation will bring you peace with God. If your heart is not changed, you can never please him.

You may have heard of Sisyphus, the mythological King of Corinth, who was condemned to roll a huge stone up a hill. Each time he reached the top, the stone rolled down and he had to start all over again. Despite expending a tremendous amount of energy, he never accomplished anything. All his best efforts

35

were in vain. There is only one thing worse than sowing in vain, building in vain or, like Sisyphus, labouring in vain, and that is to pray, fast and hear the Word of God in vain. The loss then is *eternal*!

3. Without Christ your hopes for the future are meaningless

Unless you become a Christian, there is no hope of comfort for you, either in this life or the next. The comfort of the Holy Spirit and the fear of God go together. The Lord God speaks peace only to his people (Psalm 85:8). Any sense of peace you may feel while you continue in your sins is not the true peace that comes from God. The Bible represents sin as a sickness - the worst sickness of all (Isaiah 1:5). It is like a fatal injury or a terminal disease. It pierces, wounds and torments. There is no more hope of finding true peace and comfort in your sins than there is of feeling fit and well when you are seriously ill. The fact that so many people feel that all is well with them and never cry out for the heavenly Physician serves only to underline the awful danger they are in.

Sin is a breeding-ground for all manner of diseases in the soul. Lust is a fire in the bones. Pride is a deadly inflammation. Greed is nothing less than an insatiable and unbearable thirst. Malice and envy are a poison in the heart, and so I could go on. How can anyone have any real peace and comfort with so many diseases? Only the Lord Jesus Christ can cure your sin-sick soul and give you the lasting peace that you long for. The Bible says, 'Great peace have those who love your law, and nothing causes them to stumble' (Psalm 119:165).

Real pleasure and peace come from walking in the ways of wisdom (Proverbs 3:17). Your conscience will never find peace unless it is first of all made clean (Hebrews 10:22). Any 'peace' you may feel you have while you are still living without Christ is a false peace. There are two kinds of peace which are to be dreaded more than all the troubles of the world: peace *with* sin and peace *in* sin.

Without Christ you have no hope of finding real peace in this life nor of being at peace in the life to come. You may like to think of yourself as a religious person - a Christian perhaps, but if you have never turned away from your sins and committed yourself to Jesus Christ, in Bible language you are a hypocrite. And the Bible contains some very serious warnings for hypocrites. For example, it says, 'What is the hope of the hypocrite, though he may gain much, if God takes away his life?' (Job 27:8). When a true Christian dies, all his hopes are fulfilled, but when an unbeliever dies any hopes that he entertained are entirely frustrated. When a believer is dying, his hopes are still very much alive because 'The righteous has a refuge in his death' (Proverbs 14:32). Although his body is wasting away, his hopes have every reason to flourish. His hope is a living hope, but for others it is a dying hope. The Bible says, 'When a wicked man dies, his expectation will perish and the hope of the unjust perishes' (Proverbs 11:7). Since the unsaved have hope only in this life, they are the most miserable people of all. 'The eyes of the wicked will fail, and they shall not escape. And their hope - loss of life!' (Job 11:20).

If you are hoping to be saved without Jesus Christ, you are in effect hoping to prove God a liar. The Lord himself has told you that although he is merciful and full of compassion, he will not save you if you remain as you are. He has made it plain that whoever you are and whatever you do, nothing can save you unless you become a new creature. To presume on God's mercy and to hope he will save you without your turning to Christ is to say, 'I hope God will not do as he says,' and that is a

37

blasphemous thought. The Lord *is* merciful, but he will never break his word. If your hope is worth anything it will purify you from your sins. The Bible says, 'Everyone who has this hope in him purifies himself, just as he is pure' (1 John 3:3).

4. Without Christ, the cross will be meaningless to you

Some people think that because the Lord Jesus died for sinners on the cross, then they are sure to be saved. But the truth is that Christ never died to save sinners who harden their hearts against him and persistently refuse to turn from their sins. A wise old preacher used to ask his hearers two questions: 'What has Christ done *for* you?' and 'What has the Holy Spirit done *in* you?' Unless the Holy Spirit has changed you and given you new life, the sufferings and death of Christ will be of no benefit to you.

The Bible tells us that God sent his Son into the world in order that we might be 'holy and without blame before him' (Ephesians 1:4). And when the Lord Jesus died on the cross, it was in order to 'redeem us from every lawless deed and purify for himself his own special people, zealous for good works' (Titus 2:14). If he were to save people while they continued in an ungodly life, Jesus would be setting himself against the purposes of his Father, and God himself would be going against his very nature.

God is righteous and just. He will judge each individual according to his or her works. He cannot and he will not treat the wicked and the righteous in the same way.

God is holy. It is wonderfully true that God saves sinners, but if he were to save us *in* our sins, it would cast a shadow over his holiness. The distance between God and any form of sin is immense. The Lord is infinitely pure; you can never hope to survive his judgement and stand in his presence unless he cleanses from your sins.

God is true. He has said that his anger will burn against anyone who claims to have found true peace while going his or her own way through life (Deuteronomy 29:19-20). He has also plainly declared that 'he who covers his sins will not prosper, but whoever confesses and forsakes them will have mercy' (Proverbs 28:13). The Bible teaches us that we must have clean hands and a pure heart in order to approach the Lord of heaven and earth (Psalm 24:3-4). Where would God's truth be if, despite all this, he were to save sinners without giving them a change of heart? It is surely a desperate thing to dare hope that Christ will make his own Father a liar and break his own word in order to save you.

God is wise. He will never throw away his mercy on people who will not value it, and unless you repent of your sins you will never be able to appreciate God's great salvation. You will think no more of Christ than a healthy person thinks of going to see his doctor. The One who has himself forbidden us to cast our pearls before swine will never give his best gifts to people who will merely trample them underfoot. The Lord will not dishonour himself by giving the precious blessings of heaven to sinners who find more pleasure in sin.

God never changes. He is eternally all-knowing and eternally almighty. The Lord Jesus declared that only the pure in heart will see God (Matthew 5:8). If Christ were to take anyone to heaven without first changing him inwardly, he would have to do so either without God's knowledge or against his will. Either way, it would require a change in God's character which is quite impossible.

39

If Christ were to take you to heaven while you were still in your sins, you would be quite out of place - like a fish out of water. You wouldn't fit in there. Heaven simply wouldn't suit you. After all, what does darkness have in common with light, or corruption with perfection? You wouldn't feel at home with the company in heaven and you wouldn't even enjoy the music there. If you find Sundays long and boring now, just imagine how terrible an everlasting Sunday would be!

I urge you to give up your vain hope of being saved as you are. Do you really think the laws of heaven will be reversed for you? Do you think God will change his nature for you? Do you think he will cease to be just or cease to be holy, or cease to be all-knowing and almighty just for you? Impossible! Such thoughts are absurd, not to mention blasphemous. To presume that Christ will save you as you are is to make the Saviour become a sinner.

The Lord Jesus Christ himself has said, 'Unless you are converted, you will by no means enter the kingdom of heaven' (Matthew 18:3); 'You must be born again' (John 3:7); 'Unless you repent, you will perish' (Luke 13:3). Just one word from the lips of Christ would settle the matter, but he makes the same point repeatedly and emphatically, 'Most assuredly I say to you, unless one is born again he cannot see the kingdom of God' (John 3:3). Without exception, all of us were born with a sinful nature. We must be born again by the mighty work of the Holy Spirit, or else we shall be no more fit for heaven than a wild animal is fit for the presence of a king. There is no way the Lord Jesus can go against the law of his kingdom and save you as you are. He has sworn on oath that those who are either ignorant of his ways or disobedient to them will never enter his rest (Hebrews 3:18).

40

It is important to bear in mind that God shows his hatred for sin at the same time as he shows his love to sinners. If we claim to be followers of Christ we must therefore break away from our sins and lead holy lives (2 Timothy 2:19; Titus 2:12; 1 John 3:3). The Lord Jesus wants everyone to be clear that while he pardons sin, in no way does he condone it. God has exalted him to be a Prince and Saviour (Acts 5:31); he cannot possibly save people while they are still in their sins. As King, he reigns in order to put all his enemies under his feet and to subdue the hearts of his own people. What monarch would ever take hostile rebels into his own court? If Christ is King, then he must be honoured and obeyed. And as Saviour, he demands that we turn from our sins. The very reason he was given the name 'Jesus' ('the Lord saves') is because he saves his people *from* their sins (Matthew 1:21). He not only saves from the punishment of sin, but also from its power. He is not content to do merely half the work - he is the *perfect* Saviour. God sent him to make an end of sin (Daniel 9:24) and to bless people by turning them away from their sins. You can't be saved from sin and still be content to live in sin. It's a contradiction in terms!

The time has come for you to wake up from your complacency. If you continue to live without Christ, you will go to hell. Only Jesus Christ can save you. Lay aside all your excuses. If you don't turn, you will burn. How much longer will you put it off? If you care at all about what will become of you, act now and turn to Christ. The Bible tells us about a man named Lot who lived in a region which God destroyed because of its sinfulness. On the morning of the day of reckoning, God sent some angels to urge Lot to hurry. While he was still lingering, they grabbed hold of his hand and led him out of the city and then they pleaded with him, 'Escape for your life! Do not look behind you nor stay anywhere in the plain. Escape to the mountains, lest you be destroyed' (Genesis 19:15-17). In a similar way, the Lord Jesus comes to sinners like ourselves and urges us to flee from sin. He is willing to take us by the hand and lead us away to safety. But it is vital that we are awake to our danger and to our need of his saving power.

If you continue to harden your heart against Christ, you will have only yourself to blame for your condemnation. You can't say you haven't been warned. But I cannot leave it at that. It isn't enough for me to have delivered the message that is on my heart. Will you now turn to the Saviour? Or have I been wasting my time in writing these words? I have been writing for people - for human beings with minds - not for trees and rocks. Pause and consider where you are going. Don't run into the flames of hell with your eyes open, but stop and think. Start repenting of your sins. Only a fool would allow himself to take lightly such vital matters as death, the holy anger of God and hell.

Is it reasonable to fight against the Lord your Maker? The Bible says, 'God is wise in heart and mighty in strength. Who has hardened himself against him and prospered?' (Job 9:4). Is it reasonable for you as a rational creature to reject the very purpose for which you were made? Is it reasonable for the only being in the world that God has made capable of knowing his will and bringing him glory should live in ignorance of his Creator and refuse to serve him? Judge for yourself. Could anyone, anywhere, call it reasonable? I am sure you will agree that it is absolutely unreasonable, unless you have completely taken leave of your senses. And if it is unreasonable, then there is no reason for you to continue as you are, but there is every reason in the world to immediately repent of your sins.

What more can I say? I urge you to change direction now! Would you not like to be clean? When will it happen? Sit down and think about it. Is it not best to turn to Christ? Rather than vainly trying to persuade yourself that everything will be alright in the end, why not put all your trust in the exalted Saviour? You will find him as good as his word.

O Lord God, help. Even if some of my readers will not listen to what I have written, I know that you will still hear me. I pray that those who have read these words may wake up and live! Lord, save them, or else they will be condemned. My heart would melt to see their houses on fire while they were still fast asleep in their beds, and I should be even more troubled to see them falling into everlasting punishment. Lord, have compassion and save them out of the burning. Put forth your divine power and the work will be done!

4.
The Way We Are

The Bible warns that there are very many people who do not appreciate the seriousness of their condition. They will tell you that they are very religious, they have high moral standards, all is well with them; therefore they don't need any spiritual change. But all the time they are 'a generation that is pure in its own eyes, yet is not washed from its filthiness' (Proverbs 30:12). On one occasion, the Lord Jesus sent a message to a church which considered itself spiritually rich and told it that in reality it was 'wretched, miserable, poor, blind and naked' (Revelation 3:17). We all know that looks can deceive, but so too can feelings.

With some people, it is clear for all to see that they need to be forgiven and be cleansed from their sins. The apostle Paul writes, 'For this you know, that no fornicator, unclean person, nor covetous man, who is an idolater, has any inheritance in the kingdom of Christ and God' (Ephesians 5:5). Along similar lines he wrote to the church in Corinth, 'Do you not know that the unrighteous will not inherit the kingdom of God? Do not be deceived. Neither fornicators, nor idolaters, nor adulterers, nor homosexuals, nor sodomites, nor thieves, nor covetous, nor drunkards, nor revilers, nor extortioners will inherit the kingdom of God' (1 Corinthians 6:9-10). In some of the most solemn words in the whole Bible we are told that 'the cowardly, unbelieving, abominable, murderers, sexually immoral, sorcerers, idolaters and all liars shall have their part in the lake which burns with fire and brimstone, which is the second death'

(Revelation 21:8). If you are guilty of any of the sins listed in these passages, then you require no further proof of the fact that you cannot be saved if you remain as you are.

1. Some sins are obvious

(a) Lying. The God who cannot lie has made it clear that there is no place for liars in his kingdom. 'A lying tongue' and 'a false witness who speaks lies' are among the seven sins singled out as particularly abominable to God (Proverbs 6:16-19). Liars belong with the father of lies, the devil, in hell.

(b) Swearing. The third commandment states, 'You shall not take the name of the Lord your God in vain, for the Lord will not hold him guiltless who takes his name in vain' (Exodus 20:7). If you lightly and thoughtlessly take the name of God upon your lips, whether in general conversation or in a religious oath, you are taking his name in vain. James writes, 'But above all, my brethren, do not swear, either by heaven or by earth or with any other oath. But let your "Yes" be "Yes" and your "No" "No", lest you should fall into judgement' (James 5:12).

(c) Malicious speech. The Bible repeatedly condemns cruel and spiteful words, whether spoken to another person's face or secretly behind his back. In order to enjoy fellowship with God you must be someone who 'does not backbite with his tongue, nor does evil to his neighbour, nor does he take up a reproach against his friend' (Psalm 15:1,3).

(d) Stealing. Whether it be taking advantage of your family or friends, deceiving customers for profit or so-called 'petty theft' in the workplace, the Lord is utterly opposed to all forms of stealing. He will close his door to all thieves, turning their stolen

treasures into treasures of wrath and making their ill-gotten silver and gold torment them like burning metal in their flesh (James 5:2-3).

(e) Drunkenness. The Lord God speaks against those who use alcohol in an excessive and irresponsible way: 'Woe to those who rise early in the morning, that they may follow intoxicating drink; who continue until night, till wine inflames them... Woe to men mighty at drinking wine, woe to men valiant for mixing intoxicating drink' (Isaiah 5:11,22). Such people will not inherit the kingdom of God unless they are born again and changed by the Holy Spirit.

(f) Withholding worship from God. The Lord Jesus Christ declared that the first and greatest commandment is to 'love the Lord your God with all your heart, with all your soul, with all your mind and with all your strength' (Mark 12:29-30). It follows that the first and greatest sin is to refuse to worship God, to neglect his Word, to put him out of your thoughts and to live without him.

(g) Laughing at the things of God. Contrary to what some people appear to think, there is nothing new about mocking preachers and generally ridiculing those who take the Christian faith seriously, but such laughter always comes to a tragic end as scoffers written about in the Bible discovered to their cost: 'They mocked the messengers of God, despised his words, and scoffed at his prophets, until the wrath of the Lord arose against his people, till there was no remedy' (2 Chronicles 36:16).

(h) Sexual sins. Marriage was instituted by God immediately after he had created the first man and the first woman and throughout the Bible the relationship between a man and his

46

wife is regarded as precious and worthy of universal respect. Sexual relationships belong exclusively within the marriage bond. Therefore the Bible clearly and repeatedly forbids fornication, adultery and all homosexual activity (Exodus 20:14; Leviticus 18:22; 1 Corinthians 6:9-10).

Consider carefully whether you are guilty of any of these sins. If you are, then there is no doubt that the wrath of God hangs over you and it is only a matter of time before you are condemned. You cannot run away from your conscience. And your friends, your family and your neighbours know exactly what you are like. As you walk along the road, they say, 'There goes that drunkard; there goes that scoffer; there goes that shifty dealer!' God could not have made it more plain that these are not the marks of his children. Such people will never escape hell unless the Lord changes them inwardly.

I urge you now to 'Repent and turn from all your transgressions, so that iniquity will not be your ruin' (Ezekiel 18:30). What a terrible prospect for hardened sinners! You, however, have been warned, and I am clear of your blood. Whether you take to heart what I have written or whether you choose to resist it, I shall leave the following passages of Scripture with you to serve either as thunderbolts to awaken you or as irons to harden you:

He who is often reproved and hardens his neck will suddenly be destroyed, and that without remedy (Proverbs 29:1).

Because I have called and you refused, I have stretched out my hand and no one regarded..., I will laugh at your calamity; I will mock when your terror comes, when your terror comes like a storm and your destruction comes like a whirlwind, when distress and anguish come upon you (Proverbs 1:24-27).

At this point I can imagine that many will comfort themselves with the thought that they are not guilty of any of these obvious and open sins. But that is no guarantee that all is well with you. You can deceive yourself and others and pass for a good Christian without ever having experienced the change of heart which God requires. The Lord Jesus warned that on the Day of Judgement many will say to him, "'Lord, Lord, have we not prophesied in your name, cast out demons in your name, and done many wonders in your name?" And then I will declare to them, "I never knew you; depart from me, you who practise lawlessness"' (Matthew 7:22-23). I cannot impress upon you too much the fact that thousands and millions will be condemned for some secret sin which is hidden from others and sometimes even from themselves if they do not thoroughly examine their hearts.

2. Some sins are less obvious

(a) Wilful ignorance. In Hosea 4:6, the Lord declares, 'My people are destroyed for lack of knowledge.' They were without excuse. Knowledge was available to them - God had sent his messengers, but they didn't want to know. Their ignorance was deliberate and wilful. It wasn't that they couldn't understand; they simply *wouldn't* understand. And I fear that there are many people like that today. Many of them have Bibles in their homes and even in their hands, but they stubbornly refuse to take in what their Maker is saying.

Ignorance of God and his ways is nothing to be proud of. The Bible says that when 'the Lord Jesus is revealed from heaven with his mighty angels, in flaming fire [he will take] vengeance on those who do not know God, and on those who do not obey the gospel of our Lord Jesus Christ' (2 Thessalonians 1:7-8). Make sure you are not among them - don't die of ignorance!

(b) Holding back from trusting Christ. The Lord Jesus Christ warned the crowds of people who followed him around, 'If anyone comes to me and does not hate his father and mother, wife and children, brothers and sisters, yes, and his own life also, he cannot be my disciple' (Luke 14:26). But so many people are only prepared to go so far in their religion. They never devote themselves to Christ without reservation. They love sin too much. And so they stubbornly refuse to deny themselves and count the cost of being real Christians.

(c) Religious formality. Many people are content with an outward form of religion which, while it may serve to impress other people, will lead only to their eternal ruin. They may go to church, fast, pray, give generously to good causes and genuinely believe they stand a good chance of being saved. But if they have never experienced a work of God in their hearts and if they have no personal knowledge of the life and power of the gospel of Christ, they will be condemned, despite all their hopes. It is a terrible thing if your religion serves only to harden you and to delude and deceive you.

(d) Wrong motives in religion. It is all too easy to perform 'good works' without spiritual motives. If your main motivation for engaging in religious activities is to calm your conscience, to impress other people, to gain a reputation for being a spiritual person, or to show off your various gifts and abilities, then your motives are impure and you still need a new heart.

*(e) **Trusting in your own righteousness**.* If you are trusting your own good nature to give you peace with God, you are rejecting the perfect righteousness of Christ. Strange though it may seem, your imagined 'good works' may lead to your final condemnation as much as your sins. The truth is that there is nothing you can do to turn aside God's wrath, receive forgiveness and find favour with him. And if you try to do so, you are insulting the true Saviour, Jesus Christ, by trying to make a saviour of yourself. The prophet Isaiah declares, 'We are all like an unclean thing, and all our righteousnesses are like filthy rags' (Isaiah 64:6). Like the apostle Paul, we should not boast of our own righteousness, 'but that which is through faith in Christ, the righteousness which is from God by faith' (Philippians 3:9).

*(f) **A secret aversion to Christian holiness**.* There are many people who have high moral standards and who are very precise in the practice of their religion, and yet who have no time for serious Christian discipleship. They feel very uncomfortable in the presence of people who are enthusiastic about the Lord Jesus Christ and who are zealous in his service. They regard them as fanatical extremists. Sadly, people who think in this kind of way do not place very much value on holiness for its own sake. While they may think well of themselves, in reality they are rotten at heart. A true and living faith in Christ will always lead to a longing to be like him.

*(g) **An overwhelming love of the world**.* The apostle John writes, 'If anyone loves the world, the love of the Father is not in him' (1 John 2:15). It is not uncommon for people to be guilty of this sin without being aware of it. Sometimes it is obvious to everyone else that an individual is completely absorbed with things he can see and touch while he remains oblivious to it himself. He makes all kinds of excuses for his preoccupation

50

with the things of the world and blinds himself to the truth. I am afraid that many professing Christians are more captivated by earthly things than they are by the Lord Jesus. Yet if you were to ask them, they would tell you that they value Christ above anything else. But if they stopped to examine themselves, they would soon realise that they love the world far more than they love him. The Bible says that 'those who live according to the flesh set their minds on the things of the flesh, but those who live according to the Spirit, the things of the Spirit' (Romans 8:5). If you fail to deny the cravings of your sinful nature and make it your aim to gratify your senses at all times, you are still in your sins. 'Those who are Christ's have crucified the flesh with its passions and desires' (Galatians 5:24). We are to follow the example of the apostle Paul and discipline ourselves (1 Corinthians 9:27). An inordinate love even of lawful comforts can be just as effective in keeping you from the Saviour as can the most open and ugly sins.

(h) An all-consuming thirst for revenge. Many people who claim to be Christians bear persistent grudges against those who have hurt them. But any desire to repay others for their sins is contrary to the spirit of the gospel and to the example of Christ. Where such bitterness is allowed to take root and is not hated, resisted and put to death, there is an obvious absence of the spirit of mercy and compassion which characterises the true people of God. The Lord Jesus plainly teaches that if you have experienced God's mercy in having your own sins forgiven, you will be prepared to forgive those who sin against you (Matthew 18:21-35).

(i) Unchecked pride. When men and women love to receive praise from other people more than the praise of God and set their hearts upon earning the approval of others, they are clearly strangers to the Lord Jesus. The apostle Paul testified that if he

51

still pleased men, he would not be a servant of Christ (Galatians 1:10). If you do not see the pride of your own heart and groan under it, then it is a sign that you are dead in sin.

(j) A false sense of security. Thousands, if not millions, cry 'Peace and safety!' when sudden destruction is about to come upon them. Complacency is a very great evil with disastrous consequences. Many awaken from it only when it is too late. If you imagine all that is well with you, think about what your confidence is based on. Can you identify the marks of a true believer in yourself? If you can't, you have every reason to fear your sense of peace more than you fear any amount of trouble. A false sense of security is often the most mortal enemy of the soul.

If you have stayed with me this far, I can imagine you asking, 'If all this is true, who *can* be saved?' There are many, many people who sit in churches and go through all the motions of worshipping God whose hearts are not right with him. Unless the Lord changes them, there is no hope of seeing them in heaven.

I pray that God will stir up your conscience and show you your need of mercy and forgiveness. I pray that you will not be deceived about your condition or be lulled into a false sense of security, but rather that you will see yourself as God does. I pray that you will come to see beyond any doubt whether you have received a new heart or not. If this change has taken place within you, I pray that you will recognise the difference the Lord has made to you. But if, on the other hand, you are still in a state of ignorance, prayerlessness or covetousness, I pray that you will become convinced of your sin and brought to a true and living faith in Christ.

I urge you not to deceive yourself. Let the Bible come to bear on your conscience. Listen to what God's Word says about your condition. The combined forces of a desperately wicked heart, a subtle Tempter and the deceitfulness of sin are such that it is easy to be misled. You must therefore spare no efforts in examining yourself. Do not trust your own heart. Ask the Lord to search you. If you are still not clear where you stand before God, ask a Christian friend or minister to help you. Do not give up until you are left in no doubt about your eternal welfare.

Search me, O God, and know my heart;
Try me, and know my anxieties;
And see if there is any wicked way in me,
And lead me in the way everlasting (Psalm 139:23-24).

5.
Condemned!

The condition of every non-Christian is so unspeakably desperate that I have sometimes thought that if I could only help people to see that clearly, my work would be more than half done. But I have learned from experience that unbelievers are frequently so complacent and apathetic that, even though they are prepared to admit that they have not turned to Christ, they do nothing about it. Instead, they drown out the voice of their consciences with all the responsibilities and pleasures of everyday life. The result is that they get no further than saying perhaps they will repent one day.

I am concerned therefore, not only to persuade people of their true spiritual condition, but also to impress upon them the fact that they are under God's condemnation. But immediately I am presented with a problem. Since I have never experienced the pains of hell, how can I begin to convey its terror? No mere human writer can possibly describe the full extent of the misery of a life lived without God. Even Moses, the great Old Testament prophet who spoke face to face with God, asked in prayer, 'Who knows the power of your anger?' (Psalm 90:11). The Bible tells us that sin excludes us from the presence of the Lord, but unless we have a thorough knowledge of his perfect character, we cannot appreciate just how dreadful that separation is. However, we do know enough to shake the heart of anyone who has the slightest degree of spiritual life and sense. And yet here again, I am confronted with another difficulty in that I am writing for people who may be lacking spiritual sense - people who are dead in their trespasses and sins.

Even if I could adequately represent the kingdom of heaven and all its glory, and even if it were possible to vividly describe the terrors of hell, many would simply not have the eyes to see it. Or I could write about the beauties of holiness and the glories of the gospel on the one hand, and expose the ugliness of sin on the other, but even then the spiritually colour-blind would fail to see the great distinction between the two. The Bible tells us that unbelievers have had 'their understanding darkened, being alienated from the life of God, because of the ignorance that is in them, because of the hardening of their heart' (Ephesians 4:18). They neither know, nor can know, the things of God because they lack the spiritual discernment required (1 Corinthians 2:14). They desperately need to have their eyes opened (Acts 26:18).

What shall I do to awaken such people? Shall I read their death-sentence, or ring the bell for their funeral, or tell them about the terrible judgements of God? You would think that something as sobering as that would make them tremble with fear. And yet it has no impact. They simply aren't interested. Perhaps, then, I should try speaking about the joy, the love and the good news of Jesus Christ with all his precious promises of comfort and peace? But even that would achieve nothing unless I could give people the capacity to hear as well as tell them the news.

What else could I try? Perhaps a vivid description of the lake of fire or of the glory of Christ? But that, too, is all in vain. Dead sinners are like dumb idols:

> They have mouths, but they do not speak;
> Eyes they have, but they do not see;

They have ears, but they do not hear;
Noses they have, but they do not smell;
They have hands, but they do not handle;
Feet they have, but they do not walk;
Nor do they mutter through their throat (Psalm 115:5-7).

Even if I speak the very Word of God to their hearts, it makes no impression on them. They are past feeling (Ephesians 4:19). Although God's wrath rests on them and they carry the full weight of all their sins, they live as though nothing were wrong. In a word, they carry a dead soul in a living body. Their flesh and bones are the walking coffin of a corrupt mind.

Only God can melt hardened hearts and give life and feeling to dead souls. He alone has the power to raise the dead, move mountains and bring water out of stone. He delights to work above and beyond our hopes and expectations. He can do for you what no mere man or woman can ever do. I therefore commit you to him:

O Almighty God, when you are at work, no one can stand in your way. Only you have the power to give life to the spiritually dead and to rescue them from the judgement to come. Have mercy on any readers of this book who are buried in their sins. Speak to them with words of life and make them live! Bring them light in the midst of their darkness and make them see. You are the God who formed the ear; give them the ability to hear your voice. Give them eyes to see your greatness. And give them a taste for your goodness and a sense of your beauty. Make them feel the intolerable weight of unforgiven sin, the burden of your holy anger against sin and make them appreciate the privilege of knowing your favour.

But now I must continue to explain in more detail what a terrible thing it is to be condemned by God. In doing so there

56

to what I can say because the full horror of it is so great that no one can ever describe it or understand it fully.

1. God himself is against you

That, in itself, is a dreadful thing. How terrible to be without God and without hope in the world! Without him, where can you turn for help? In a time of crisis, where will you look? When the time comes for you to leave this world and to say good-bye to your friends, your family and all your possessions, what will you do if you have no God to go to? Will you still try to call to him for help? If you do, he will not recognise you. He will take no notice of you, but will declare, 'I never knew you; depart from me, you who practise lawlessness' (Matthew 7:23).

Left to yourself, you are not only without God, but God is against you. If he were neutral your position would not be half so bad, even if he didn't do anything to positively help you. Or if he were to hand you over to evil people and allow the devil to do his worst to you, it would still be better than to have the Lord himself against you. The Bible says, 'It is a fearful thing to fall into the hands of the living God' (Hebrews 10:31). There is no friend like him, and there is no enemy like him either. There is nothing worse than to have the Almighty as your tormentor and to be punished with everlasting destruction from the presence of the Lord himself (2 Thessalonians 1:9).

If God is against you, who shall be for you? In the words of the Bible, 'If one man sins against another, God will judge him. But if a man sins against the Lord, who will intercede for him?' (1 Samuel 2:25). Addressing God, the psalmist says, 'You, yourself, are to be feared; and who may stand in your presence when once you are angry?' (Psalm 76:7). Who can rescue you from God's anger? Money can't - 'Riches do not profit in the

57

day of wrath' (Proverbs 11:4). Neither can kings and armies - 'The kings of the earth, the great men, the rich men, the commanders, the mighty men, every slave and every free man [will hide themselves] in the caves and in the rocks of the mountains and [will say] to the mountains and rocks, "Fall on us and hide us from the face of him who sits on the throne and from the wrath of the Lamb! For the great day of his wrath has come, and who is able to stand?"' (Revelation 6:15-17).

The thought of having the Lord as your enemy should pierce your heart. Where will you go for refuge? There is no hope for you unless you lay down your weapons and ask Christ to stand as your friend and to make peace between you and God. Without this, you might as well take yourself off to a lonely place and give full vent to your despair and anguish of heart. But in Jesus Christ there is a possibility of mercy for you. More than that, there is an *offer* of mercy. You can have God more for you than he is currently against you. But if you will not leave your sins behind and turn to him with all your heart, his holy anger remains on you. In fact every aspect of his character is against you:

(a) God's face is against you. 'The face of the Lord is against those who do evil' (Psalm 34:16). God's very heart is turned against you. Doesn't that make you tremble?

(b) God's justice is against you. The Lord declares, '[I will] sharpen my flashing sword and my hand grasps it in judgement, I will take vengeance on my adversaries, and repay those who hate me' (Deuteronomy 32:41 NIV). God's justice is so precise that he will by no means clear the guilty. Unless you are looking to Christ to save you, you will have to pay the penalty for your own sins. When you begin to appreciate the justice of God and the standard by which you will be judged, you experience

58

something like an earthquake in your soul. The tragedy is that the devil will do his utmost to hide such realities from you. He will try to persuade you that the Lord is nothing but mercy. He will tell you there is nothing to be worried about and encourage you to feel comfortable in your sins. But the truth is that God is exact in his judgement. Every single sin must be paid for. The Lord has promised to send 'indignation and wrath, tribulation and anguish, on every soul of man who does evil' - on all 'who are self-seeking and do not obey the truth, but obey unrighteousness' (Romans 2:8). 'Cursed is everyone who does not continue in all things which are written in the book of the law to do them' (Galatians 3:10).

If you think it is a terrible thing for a bankrupt debtor to come face to face with his creditor, just think how much worse it is for an unforgiven sinner to meet God. The face of God to a bankrupt sinner is more terrible than the face of a judge to a criminal or the sight of the electric chair to the murderer who has been sentenced to death. 'Bind him hand and foot, take him away, and cast him into darkness; there will be weeping and gnashing of teeth' (Matthew 22:13). 'Depart from me, you cursed, into the everlasting fire prepared for the devil and his angels' (Matthew 25:41). This is the terrible sentence that justice pronounces. And unless you repent and trust the Lord Jesus Christ, these are the words that will ring in your ears on that last and terrible day of judgement.

(c) God's holiness is against you. God's whole nature is infinitely and eternally opposed to all sin. There is no way he can take delight in any sinner who is separated from Christ. True, God is angry with his own children when they disobey him, but when it comes to those who have never turned from their sins, his displeasure is fixed and constant.

59

What a miserable thing to be out of God's favour! Unless you yourself are changed, the Lord can no more change his attitude towards you than he can change his nature and no longer be God. He is a great and glorious God. Even the stars are not pure in his sight (Job 25:5). He has to humble himself to look at things in heaven itself (Psalm 113:6). His eyes are all-searching. If you have never trusted Christ, what good can he possibly see in you? Surely you should be crying out, 'Who is able to stand before this holy Lord God?' (1 Samuel 6:20).

(d) God's power is against you. The Bible tells us that the glory of God's power will be displayed in the destruction of those who do not obey the good news of Jesus Christ (2 Thessalonians 1:8-9). The power of God's anger is against you like a mighty cannon. It is a terrifying combination - power and anger. It would be better to have all the armies of the world arrayed against you than to be confronted by the power of God. You can never hope to escape from his hands, and there is no release from his prison. 'The thunder of his power who can understand?' (Job 26:14). Don't hold out against the Lord until you understand it by bitter experience! The Bible declares:

> God is wise in heart and mighty in strength.
> Who has hardened himself against him and prospered?
> He removes the mountains, and they do not know when he
>   overturns them in his anger;
> He shakes the earth out of its place, and its pillars tremble;
> He commands the sun and it does not rise;
> He seals off the stars;
> He alone spreads out the heavens,
> And treads on the waves of the sea...
> Who can say to him, 'What are you doing?'
> God will not withdraw his anger,
> The allies of the proud lie prostrate before him
>   (Job 9:4-8, 12-13).

60

Do you really consider yourself able to take on God? The Lord declares, 'Now consider this, you who forget God, lest I tear you in pieces and there be none to deliver' (Psalm 50:22). I appeal to you to submit now to the mercy of God. No creature of dust can ever hope to defeat the Almighty. The Bible says, 'Woe to him who strives with his Maker' (Isaiah 45:9). The Lord can easily destroy every puny 'weapon' you may attempt to use in your opposition to him. Don't even try! Rather, lay down your weapons and make peace with him. Don't wait to feel the full power of his anger against you, but trust in his mighty power to save you.

(e) God's wisdom is against you. The all-wise God has already prepared for the day of reckoning. The Bible tells us very plainly:

> God is a just judge,
> And God is angry with the wicked every day.
> If he does not turn back,
> He will sharpen his sword:
> He bends his bow and makes it ready.
> He also prepares for himself instruments of death;
> He makes his arrows into fiery shafts (Psalm 7:11-13).

God in his infinite wisdom has carefully planned everything, right down to the final detail.

(f) God's truth is against you. If the Lord is faithful and true to his word, then he will certainly condemn you if you continue as you are. Unless you repent, you will die eternally. The Bible is crystal clear on this point: 'If we are faithless, he remains faithful; he cannot deny himself' (2 Timothy 2:13). The Lord is faithful in his threatenings as well as in his promises. And if you do not believe, he will demonstrate his faithfulness in your

61

destruction. The faithfulness of God is of great comfort to believers, but to unbelievers it is to be feared.

What, then, do you think of what God's Word says to you? Do you believe these threatenings and warnings or not? If you reject them out of hand, there is no hope for you. But if you do believe them, how can you carry on as you are in the sure knowledge that every part of God's nature is opposed to you? The whole book of God is united in its testimony against you while you remain in your sins. Every single page condemns you. And the Lord Jesus Christ has declared that, 'Till heaven and earth pass away, one jot or one tittle will by no means pass from the law till all is fulfilled' (Matthew 5:18).

What are you going to do? Where will you flee? The Lord is everywhere and he knows everything - you cannot hope to run away from him. He is committed to keeping his word, so without question you will be condemned unless you repent and turn to Christ. And if God has almighty power to torment you, then you will be miserable for ever unless you find peace with him now while there is still time.

2. The whole of God's creation is against you

In the New Testament, the apostle Paul depicts the whole creation as groaning and labouring with birth pangs because of the way it is persistently treated by sinful people (Romans 8:22). After generations of being abused to serve the selfish desires of sinners, the world that God has made longs for relief. So, if the trees, plants, flowers, land and sea were able to speak and reason, they would cry out in protest at the way they are being treated contrary to their natures and to the purpose for which God made them. As someone has said, 'If alcohol had the capacity to know how it is abused by the drunkard, it would groan against him in the barrel, in his cup, in his throat and in his stomach. If it could speak, it would confront him to his face. Every creature in the world would groan against unbelieving men and women if only it had the necessary powers of reason. The ground would groan to support you, the air would groan to give you breath, your bed would groan to give you rest, your food would groan to nourish you and your clothes would groan to cover you. Everything would rise up in protest at having to give you any help or comfort while you continue to live in sin against God.'

It is a solemn thought to consider that you are a burden to creation. If inanimate creatures could speak, the food on your plate would cry out to God, 'Lord, must I nourish this person and give him strength to dishonour you? If you would only give me permission, I would choke him!' The very air that you breathe would say, 'Lord, must I give this woman breath so that she can blaspheme your name, insult your people and engage in corrupt speech? Just give the word and I will make sure she never breathes again.' Even your regular means of transport would complain, 'Lord, must I help him on his way to commit yet more sins against you?' If you do not belong to Jesus Christ, the earth groans *under* you and hell groans *for* you until death shall satisfy both. While the Lord remains against you, you can be sure that all his creatures - in heaven and on earth - are against you. You cannot be at peace with what God has made if you have not found peace with God himself.

3. Satan has full power over you

If you do not belong to Christ, you are securely held in the grip of the devil - that roaring lion who is ever greedy to devour you (1 Peter 5:8). You are trapped in 'the snare of the devil, having been taken captive by him to do his will' (2 Timothy 2:26). The been taken captive by him to do his will' (2 Timothy 2:26). The Bible describes the devil as 'the ruler of the darkness of this world' (Ephesians 6:12). In other words, every man, woman, boy or girl who lives in the darkness and ignorance of sin is under the rule and dominion of the devil. The devil is his or her god. Not that they intend to worship him necessarily; indeed, they may be offended by the suggestion. Nevertheless, the Bible states very plainly that 'you are slaves of the one whom you obey' (Romans 6:16). On the final day of judgement, many who had considered themselves children of God will be condemned as servants of the devil. As soon as he suggests some sinful pleasure to you, you embrace the opportunity. If he suggests a lie or prompts you to get even with somebody, you readily obey. If he tries to persuade you not to read the Bible or pray, you listen to him. That is what I mean when I say you are a servant of the devil if you do not belong to Jesus Christ. Of course, Satan does not introduce himself and you may not be aware of the source of the temptations that come your way. He stands behind the curtain as it were and acts in the dark. When you lie, for example, you are probably not consciously serving the devil; you are merely seeking your own advantage. But it is Satan who puts the thought into your heart. When Judas Iscariot betrayed the Lord Jesus for thirty pieces of silver, it is unlikely that he knew he was following the promptings of the devil. Some people fool themselves into thinking they are free when all the time they are unwittingly obeying the devil.

Have you turned from the darkness of sin to the light of Christ? If not, I fear that you are under the power of Satan. Are you consciously and deliberately sinning against God? That, too, is a sign that you belong to the devil. I do not deny for a moment that Satan liberally supplies his servants with all kinds of pleasures, but his motive is only and always to bring you to eternal misery. He may approach you laden with attractive to conceal his deadly sting. The one who is now your tempter will one day be your tormentor. If only I could make you see what a bad master you are serving! He is a merciless tyrant who is set on making your condemnation sure and heating the furnace ever hotter in which you must burn for millions and millions of years.

4. The guilt of all your sins lies like a mountain on top of you

You may not feel it, but if you have not turned to Christ all your sins are held against you. Not one of them has been blotted out. The forgiveness of sins and a change of heart go together. You can't have one without the other. If your heart does not belong to the Lord Jesus, you are not right with God, and if you are not right with God, you are still in your sins. It is a terrible thing to be in debt, but the worst debt of all is to be in debt to God. There is no arrest so formidable and no prison so dreary as his. When the Lord wakes you up to feel the weight of your guilt, you become restless and uncomfortable. You begin to envy the stones in the street because they cannot feel what you feel. You may even wish you had been created a dog rather than a human being made in the image of God because at least then death would bring an end to your misery. But as it is, death will be just the beginning of a misery that will never end.

No matter how much you try to laugh it off now, one day you will find the guilt of unforgiven sin a burden greater than you can bear. Don't forget that it was the guilt of our sins which caused the agony and death of the Lord Jesus Christ. There is nothing trivial about sin.

Once again I urge you to stop and think while there is still time. When you hear the Lord Jesus say to you, 'You shall die in your sins' (John 8:24), don't you tremble? If death could take away

65

all your sins as well as all your comforts, it would not be half as bad. But the fact is that your sins will follow you when your friends forsake you and when everything you have ever enjoyed on earth will fade away. Your sins will not die with you, but they will go to judgement with you and accuse you. And then they will go to hell with you to torment you for ever. You can never hope to repay your debts to God. Every one of God's commandments is ready to arrest you and take you by the throat. What will you do? There is only one thing to do! Despair of yourself and flee to Christ. He is your only hope.

5. You are a slave to sin

Until you receive the mercy of God, sin reigns over you and holds you under its dominion. There is no tyrant quite like sin for the perverse nature of the work it demands of its slaves. If you are anything like me, it would break your heart to see a company of men and women struggling to gather fuel for a fire on which they will be burned to death. But that is precisely the kind of work in which the slaves of sin are constantly engaged. Even while they congratulate themselves on the riches they have amassed through their sins and rejoice in the fruits of their dubious labours, they are treasuring up vengeance for their eternal burning. They are adding to the pile of judgement and pouring oil upon it in order to make the flame rage even fiercer. Who wants to serve a master whose work is drudgery and whose wages are death?

One of the saddest scenes portrayed in the New Testament is of a demon-possessed man who lived among the tombs, cutting and wounding himself. That is what it is like to be a slave of sin. Every action you perform is like another thrust at your throat. While your conscience is asleep you may not be aware of it, but

66

once death and judgement bring you to your senses, you will feel the pain of every wound. The terrible bondage of sin is perhaps most clearly seen in people who have been awakened to see the condition they are in, yet who persist in their sins. Their consciences are alive and active and they are left in no doubt as to where their sins will lead them and yet they are held in such a miserable slavery that on they go. Faced with temptation, they cast aside all their good intentions and resolutions and are carried headlong to their own destruction.

6. The fires of hell are ready for you

The prophet Isaiah depicts hell and destruction with an open mouth groaning for you, waiting as it were with a greedy eye as you stand on the brink (Isaiah 5:14). If the wrath of a mere man is 'like the roaring of a lion' (Proverbs 19:12) and more heavy than sand (Proverbs 27:3), who can imagine what the wrath of the infinite God is like? In the Bible, King Nebuchadnezzar commanded that the fiery furnace for execution be made seven times hotter with the effect that it consumed even those who went near it to throw in three despised Israelites. How much more fierce is the fury of the Almighty God! How dreadful to be a faggot in hell for all eternity! Listen to the words of the Lord God himself: 'Can your heart endure, or can your hands remain strong in the days when I shall deal with you?' (Ezekiel 22:14). Can you bear the thought of everlasting burnings? Could you put up with being like a glowing iron in hell, with your whole body and soul possessed by God's burning vengeance? How will you endure when the Lord sets himself against you to torment you, when your conscience serves as a channel for his eternal wrath and when you shall be as full of suffering as you are now full of sin? In such a state, you will lament your immortality and vainly long to be annihilated.

67

For the time being, you may try to laugh and be happy and put out of your mind any thought of the terrors of the Lord. But it will be quite a different story when you shall 'lie down in torment' (Isaiah 50:11); when roarings and blasphemies shall be your only music, and 'the wine of the wrath of God, which is poured out in full strength into the cup of indignation' shall be your only drink (Revelation 14:10). The smoke of your torment shall ascend for ever and ever and you shall have no rest during the day or night - no rest in your conscience and no relief in your body.

Pause and consider! Think of where you are standing - right on the brink of destruction. You are only one short step away from condemnation. When you lie down to sleep tonight you have no guarantee that you won't wake up in hell tomorrow morning. And when you get up in the morning, you cannot be sure where you will be by the time the sun sets. Dare you laugh it off? Will you carry on as you are as if there were nothing wrong? If you are thinking to yourself that none of this applies to you, look over the previous chapter again. Can you really say you are innocent of every one of those sins? Don't close your eyes to the truth. Don't deceive yourself. Acknowledge the desperate condition you are in while there is still time to do something about it. Just think what it is like to be a vile outcast, to be for ever lost, to be eternally consumed by the burning wrath of a holy God. God's wrath is a fierce, devouring, everlasting, unquenchable fire and it will be poured out upon you unless you turn to the Lord with all your heart.

If I were to flatter you, I wouldn't be doing you any favours at all. Rather I would be helping you on your way to the unquenchable fire. God's wrath can no more come to an end than immortality can die, immutability change, eternity run out

68

or omnipotence lose its power. The living God himself declares that hell awaits you - unless he changes you by his grace.

7. The whole Bible testifies against you

God's law thunders against you. It cries out for justice. But it is not just the law; the gospel also condemns you. Listen to the words of the New Testament: 'He who does not believe will be condemned' (Mark 16:16); 'Unless you repent, you will all likewise perish' (Luke 13:3); 'This is the condemnation, that the light has come into the world, and men loved darkness rather than light because their deeds were evil' (John 3:19); 'He who does not believe...shall not see life, but the wrath of God abides on him' (John 3:36); 'If the word spoken by angels proved steadfast, and every transgression and disobedience received a just reward, how shall we escape if we neglect so great a salvation?' (Hebrews 2:2-3); 'Anyone who has rejected Moses' law dies without mercy on the testimony of two or three witnesses. Of how much worse punishment will he be thought worthy who has trampled the Son of God underfoot?' (Hebrews 10:28-29).

All these words are as true as the God who spoke them. It is far better for you to open your eyes now, while you can still do something about your predicament, rather than harden yourself until, to your eternal sorrow, you will experience the judgement you refused to believe. Why are you still holding back? What keeps you from believing? Sin must have robbed you of your reason and left you incapable of looking after your own eternal interests. You have been drugged by folly. What can I do to bring you to your senses?

The Lord has given you a mind and the ability to reason. Have you forgotten that you will live for ever - either in heaven or in

69

hell? If you acknowledge that fact, how can you possibly be so casual about the prospect of an eternity of misery? What could be more unreasonable? Yet if that is your attitude, you have not merely taken leave of your senses, but you are acting in complete opposition to one of the most precious faculties with which God has blessed you. Why will you not pause to consider where you will spend eternity? It is only a matter of time before you die. The Judge of all the earth is ready to call you to account. In a short while, time will be no more. Are you really prepared to run the risk of going to hell because you don't want to think seriously about what God says to you? For your own sake, stop and think!

Listen to what the Lord says: 'Do you not fear me? Will you not tremble at my presence?' (Jeremiah 5:22). Don't take the wrath of God lightly. A time is coming when you will certainly not be able to shrug it off. Even the devils believe and tremble! Are you more hardened than they are? How much longer will you run along the precipice? Will you continue to play with fire? How can you be indifferent to whether you endure God's wrath or escape it? No one is more senseless than the person who:

> [Stretches] out his hand against God,
> And acts defiantly against the Almighty,
> Running stubbornly against him
> With his strong embossed shield (Job 15:25-26).

How can it be wise to play around on the brink of the lake of fire? What more can I say? I cannot think of any expression or image which adequately conveys the sheer madness of continuing in a sinful life. I urge you, therefore to wake up and live! There is only one way of escape - and that is through Jesus Christ. Turn from your sins. Come to Christ. Receive his righteousness. Acknowledge him as your only Lord and Master. Begin to live

70

a new life. Because if you don't, you will be condemned to hell. Think again of the plight you are in. Surely the matter of your eternal misery or bliss is worthy of careful consideration? Think again about the awful condemnation that awaits you. By all means ignore everything I have written if it doesn't tie up with what God has revealed in the Bible. But if what I have written is true, what a terrible state you are in! Common sense dictates that you take all necessary steps to escape the dreadful judgement which will otherwise surely come upon you.

Why is it that in matters connected with your home or your career, you are very quick to foresee difficulties and readily take all necessary precautions to avoid them, but when it comes to matters relating to your eternal destiny, you are much more careless? Doesn't it mean anything to you to have the infinite God against you? Do you think you can live without his favour? Do you really imagine you can escape his hands or endure his vengeance? Can you hear the whole of creation groaning under you, and hell groaning for you - and still feel confident that you will make it to heaven? Are you comfortable with the thought that as a slave of sin you are building up an even greater weight of judgement for yourself with every breath you take? Will you dismiss the threatenings of God's law as if they had been spoken by an uneducated child? Do you merely laugh at hell?

I want to speak very plainly to you. Are you really so proud as to think you can resist your Maker? To listen to some people talk, you would think that God's arrows were made of grass. They speak and act as though the Almighty couldn't hurt a fly. The arrogance of it! There is nothing to laugh at and everything to fear. And if the warnings and promises of the Bible will not awaken you, death and judgement certainly will. What will you do when the Lord comes against you in his holy anger, and the words you have been reading in this book become your

71

words you have been reading in this book become your experience? In the Bible, when Daniel's enemies, together with their wives and children, were thrown into the lions' den, all their bones were broken into pieces before they even reached the ground. Don't imagine you will escape more lightly than that when you fall into the hands of the living God.

Give up your fight with God. Repent and be converted and then none of these things shall happen to you.

> Seek the Lord while he may be found,
> Call upon him while he is near.
> Let the wicked forsake his way,
> And the unrighteous man his thoughts;
> Let him return to the Lord,
> And he will have mercy on him;
> And to our God,
> For he will abundantly pardon (Isaiah 55:6-7).

6.
What must I do?

Before you read this chapter, I want to urge you to make up your mind to do whatever God in his Word requires of you. In the words of the Bible itself, I plead with you to 'Set your hearts on all the words which I testify among you today... For it is not a futile thing for you - it is your life' (Deuteronomy 32:46). Everything I have written so far has been leading to this appeal that you allow nothing to keep you from a wholehearted turning to God. I would not have troubled you with thoughts of your eternal misery and condemnation if there were no hope of escape for you. If nothing could be done, kindness would have dictated that I leave you alone so that you could enjoy the brief pleasures this life has to offer in relative peace. But something *can* be done. You *can* be eternally happy - so long as you accept God's rescue plan. In this section I shall direct you to the open door of God's mercy. All you have to do is rise up and enter through it. I want to show you the way of life so that you may walk in it, and live and not die.

If you are condemned in the end, you have only yourself to blame. You have chosen to follow the path that leads to destruction. Your Creator calls you to turn from your sins and Christian men and women everywhere echo his cry. Yet sadly, in many cases, the message falls on deaf ears. No amount of reasoning, warning, persuasion and pleading makes any impact as people press headlong into eternal misery.

If you had in your possession an infallible cure for some fatal disease that was sweeping through the country, how would you feel if it continued to claim the lives of your friends and neighbours simply because they refused to receive the treatment that would save them? Surely even the hardest heart with some trace of humanity remaining in it would be grieved. How senseless and foolish! Yet there are thousands and millions of people just like that when it comes to their eternal salvation. The symptoms of eternal death are clearly evident, yet they refuse God's prescription. In this chapter I propose to issue the prescription that the Lord has written down in the Bible. It is a prescription which guarantees a certain cure. Follow these directions and you shall be saved.

1. Admit that you cannot get to heaven as you are

You must be very clear in your mind on this first point. Unless God changes you inwardly, you will never enter heaven. Only Christ can save you and he tells you that you must be born again. You must receive new life from God. The Lord Jesus Christ holds the keys to heaven. There is no back entrance;
you have to go through him. And he will never admit you into God's holy presence unless you experience a spiritual change.

2. Be clear about your sinfulness

Until you become sick and weary of your sins, you will not come to the Saviour for a cure. You need to feel the weight of your sins and develop a conscience that is sensitive to sin. You will never come to Christ for life if you have not first of all seen yourself as dead. I urge you, therefore, to examine yourself thoroughly so that you will appreciate more fully the depth and extent of your sinfulness. Ask for the help of God's Spirit to convince you of your sin. Let your conscience get to work until you are brought low before God.

Think about *the number* of sins you are guilty of. The heart of Israel's King David fainted when he stopped to consider just how numerous his sins were. His discovery that he had more sins in his heart than hairs upon his head made him cry out to God for mercy. Sinful desires fill the head, heart, eyes and mouth like maggots on a dead carcass. Cast your mind back for a moment: was there ever a place or a time when you did not sin? Take a look within: what part of your character is not poisoned by sin and what duty do you ever perform which is completely free from sin's poison? Your total debt to God is incalculable and you cannot repay a single penny. Call to mind the sins you have committed and all the good that you have failed to do; the sins of your thoughts, your words and your actions; the sins of your youth and the sins of your older years. Don't be like the bankrupt who is afraid to review his accounts. Read the records of conscience with care; they will surely be examined sooner or later.

Think about *the seriousness* of sin. Each and every sin is an enemy of the God of your life and of the life of your soul. All sin is an expression of opposition to his law, his warnings and his mercy. Never underestimate the havoc that sin has caused. It has brought death into the world; it has robbed and enslaved people; it has turned the world upside down; it has produced conflict between the human race and the animal kingdom and within the human race itself. In each individual man, woman, boy and girl, sin has set passion against reason, the will against judgement and lust against conscience. Sin is the ultimate cause of all sickness, all human misery, all boredom and drudgery, all marriage breakdown and divorce, and all wars. Worst of all, it has destroyed fellowship with our Maker, leaving us all both hateful to God and haters of God. In view of all this, how could anyone possibly view sin as a trivial matter?

Sin is the traitor that thirsted for the blood of the Son of God. It sold him, mocked him, scourged him, spat in his face, tore his hands, pierced his side, crushed his soul, mangled his body and had him bound, condemned, nailed, crucified and exposed to public humiliation. It is such a deadly poison that just one drop applied to the root of humanity has corrupted, spoiled, poisoned and ruined the entire race. As a bloodthirsty executioner, sin has killed prophets, burned martyrs, murdered apostles, patriarchs and monarchs, destroyed cities, swallowed empires and devoured nations. The weapons employed may have varied from place to place, but the force behind it all was the same in every case. How could anyone say that sin is of little consequence? If the human remains of everyone who has ever lived could be recovered and an inquest could be made into the identity of the murderer who was guilty of every death, sin would be found guilty without exception. Reflect on the nature of sin until your heart is inclined to fear it and hate it. Consider how you have sinned against God's warnings, against his kindness and love, against the light you have received, against your own resolutions and promises, even against your own prayers. Don't put any of it out of your mind until you blush with shame and you are shaken out of your complacency.

Think about what sin *deserves*. It cries out to heaven for vengeance. There is no question that its condemnation has been well earned. It brings God's curse upon both soul and body. If even the least sinful word or thought makes you the object of his infinite wrath, just think what a weight of judgement you deserve for your many thousands of sins! Please, I urge you, judge yourself in order that the Lord may not judge you.

Think about the *ugliness* of sin. You would be appalled if you could see yourself in all the terrible deformity of your nature.

Sin is more polluted than any sewer and more to be feared than any cancer. Think about the most repulsive thing you can imagine. What would really turn your stomach? Whatever you have come up with, you can be quite sure that the revulsion you feel is nothing compared with what the holy and glorious God feels about sin. And until you have been made clean by the blood of Jesus and received a new heart, your sins are an offence to him.

Think about two sins in particular:

(a) The sin of your heart. If the roots of a tree are rotten, there is no point pruning the branches. Something more radical needs to be done. And it is the same with you; you need to get to the source of your sinfulness. Consider how deeply-rooted it is and how it spreads through your whole being. Everything that keeps you from doing right and everything that inclines you to do wrong can be traced back to your sinful heart. How do spiritual blindness, pride, prejudice and unbelief enter your mind? What makes you resist the Lord so stubbornly? What makes you so fickle in your feelings towards God? Why is your conscience so insensitive and unreliable? And why are you so slow to remember what the Lord has said? The answer lies in your heart. Your sinful heart has put every part of your soul out of order. It has filled your head with evil plans, your hands with sinful practices, your eyes with covetousness and your tongue with bitter poison. It has also opened your ears to lies and unclean talk and closed them to the words of life. Can you still take pride in yourself and say you are good at heart? Let these thoughts roll over in your mind until you are humbled before God and brought to repentance.

(b) Your own besetting sin - the sin you are most addicted to. I urge you to put away your fond thoughts of it. Recognise it for

the ugly, hateful thing it is. Remember what the Holy One says about it. Make it your top priority to repent of this particular sin. Guard against it. It is dishonouring to God and dangerous to you.

3. Wake up to the desperate condition you are in

Read over the previous chapter again and again. Get it out of the book and into your heart. When you lie down to sleep at night, for all you know you may wake up in flames. And when you get up in the morning, there is no guarantee that before the sun sets you may be making your bed in hell. You are tottering right on the brink of the bottomless pit. How can you possibly be content to carry on living in such a dreadful predicament? Imagine you saw someone condemned to die, hanging over a fiery furnace, suspended by nothing more than a thin thread, ready to break at any moment. Wouldn't your heart go out to him? Yet if you are not trusting the Lord Jesus Christ, that is precisely the situation in which you find yourself. Where would you be if the thread of your life were to break - and it could happen at any moment. Where would you drop? If you remain as you are, you would fall into the lake of fire where you must suffer for as long as God is God. Doesn't that make you tremble? If even this fails to move you, you must have lost all love for yourself as well as for the Lord.

Reflect on these things until your heart calls out for Christ as earnestly as a drowning man cries out for a lifeboat. So long as you do not see the seriousness of your sins, you will never appreciate your serious need of the Saviour. You need to be brought to an end of yourself. Until then, there is little hope for you. It is far better for you to fear the punishment that awaits you now, rather than to experience it later. So don't attempt to suppress your conscience and don't try to put out of your mind any thoughts of the judgement to come. It may well be necessary for you to experience some painful pangs of conscience in order to lead you to the cure that only the Lord Jesus Christ can give.

4. Look away from yourself

There is nothing you can do to save yourself. Reading the Bible, listening to preaching, praying and making good resolutions will never take away your sins. There is, of course, a place for all these things, but don't pin your hopes on them. Only Jesus Christ can save you. Nothing and no one else will do. You must therefore renounce any hopes you may be cherishing of saving yourself by your own wisdom, your own good works or your own strength. People who are trusting their own efforts won't ask Christ to save them. They don't see the point. That is why you need to recognise your imagined wisdom as folly, your righteousness as rags and rottenness and your strength as weakness. You can no more save yourself than a dead body can shake off its graveclothes and spring back to life.

So when you pray to the Lord and meditate on his Word, or follow any of the directions contained in this chapter, you must look away from yourself and ask God for the help of the Holy Spirit. In your own strength you cannot do anything to make yourself acceptable to God, but that is no excuse for neglecting to do your duty. The Bible tells us how the Lord sent a messenger to the Ethiopian Chancellor of the Exchequer at the very time he was reading the Word of God (Acts 8:29-30). The Holy Spirit came upon the first disciples of Jesus while they were praying (Acts 2:1-4), and later Cornelius and his friends were filled with the Holy Spirit while listening to the preaching of God's Word (Acts 10:44).

5. Turn your back on all your sins

You are entertaining false hopes if you imagine you can receive new life from Christ while you are still clinging to your sins. If you don't leave your sins behind, you cannot find mercy. You can't be joined to the Lord Jesus unless you have made a definite and decisive break with sin. There is no other way of finding peace with God. You must either part with your sins or part with your soul. If you spare just one sin, the Lord will not spare you. Either your sins must die, or you must die for your sins. Perhaps you are thinking that God will excuse you if you hold onto just one pet sin - just a little one, a secret one. After all, you tell yourself, it doesn't really do anyone else any harm; in fact no one else need know it is even there. But no! The Lord says that this single sin is enough to cost you the life of your soul, no matter how much you may try to defend it with your excuses.

Consider these things very carefully. If you give up your sins, God will give you his Christ, the Saviour. Is that not a fair exchange? If you die in your sins and go to hell, it will not be because God has never provided a Saviour for sinners and it will not be because you never knew the way to life. It will be for one reason only: because you preferred sin to Christ - the murderer to the Saviour. Take time to examine yourself. Ask yourself, What sins am I guilty of? Where have I failed in my duty towards God? How have I sinned against other people? Having exposed your sins in this manner, make up your mind to have nothing more to do with them. Regard them as a deadly poison - to be thrown out for ever. After all, why should you want to hold onto them? While they may offer you some degree of pleasure for a time, they will never do you any real and lasting good. All the time they are stirring up God's justice and anger against you. They will open hell to you and pile up the fuel to burn you. You have been betrayed by sin. Don't now let your

80

betrayer go on to execute you. Instead, make up your mind to put sin itself to death. Turn away from your sins and let Christ be your Lord.

6. Acknowledge God as your God

You have a simple choice to make. On the one hand there is the world with all you can see, hear, touch and taste, and on the other hand there is the glorious and infinitely holy God. There is no comparison between the two. Only God can satisfy your deepest needs and only he can give you true and lasting joy. The Lord is greater than all the world in every possible way. If you make him *your* God, you have every reason to be content. Other people may opt for the riches and pleasures of the world, but make sure you put finding favour with God first.

Let me remind you again that you have turned away from the Lord; you have incurred his wrath and yet, through Jesus Christ, he stands ready to be your God once again. How do you respond to his gracious offer? Will you acknowledge the Lord as your God? If you are wise, you will. Come to him through Jesus Christ. Turn your back on your love of money, pleasure and reputation. Throw them off the throne of your heart and let God be your Lord and King. It's all or nothing. The only true God cannot tolerate any other master; he must come first in your life.

(a) Accept God as he is - Father, Son and Holy Spirit

Acknowledge God the Father as your Father. Come to him and say, 'Father, I have sinned against heaven and in your sight, and I am not worthy to be called your son. I deserve nothing from you at all and yet, since you are so gracious and kind and full of mercy, I am coming to you and I ask you to receive me. I come

81

with all the simplicity of a child and entrust myself to your care. I cast all my burdens on you and ask you to guide me and direct my life. I submit myself to your discipline and correction and commit all my needs into your hands. I am giving up all my self-confidence and pride; from now on my trust is in you. I want to belong to you and to no one else.'

Receive God the Son, the Lord Jesus Christ, as your Saviour. Accept him as the only way to the Father and the only source of spiritual life. He is the righteousness you so desperately need. Say to him, 'Lord, I am yours. Everything that I am and all that I have belongs to you - my body, my soul and all my possessions. I give you my heart; I want to be undividedly and everlastingly devoted to you. From this day on, I will regard everything I possess as belonging to you. I want no other king to rule over me apart from you. In the past I have obeyed other voices, but now I commit myself to serving you alone. I utterly reject my own righteousness; I despair of ever being forgiven and saved by my own feeble efforts, and I look to you for pardon, life and acceptance with God. Only your sacrifice can atone for my sins and only your intercession can prevail before his throne. I submit to you as my divine Teacher and Lord and stand ready to do your will.'

Welcome God the Holy Spirit as the One who will make you holy and more like Christ. He will give you wisdom, strength, comfort and understanding. Present yourself as a temple for him. Open wide your heart to receive him. Surrender to his control every faculty of your soul and consecrate to him every part of your body in order that you may do the will of God.

(b) Accept God as he has revealed himself

In the Bible, the Lord has shown himself to be a merciful and gracious God who forgives the sins of everyone who turns to him. There is no better news than that! You might think that any sinner would want such a God because without him there is no hope for any of us. But there is much more to the Lord than that. 'Yes,' he says, 'I am forgiving, but I am also holy and I hate sin with an intense hatred. If you want to be one of my people, you must be holy yourself - holy in heart and holy in life. You must put away all your sins - no matter how much you love them, no matter how natural they may seem to you and no matter how much you may feel you 'need' them. Unless sin becomes your enemy, I cannot be your God.' How do you respond? 'Lord, I want to share in your holiness. I love you, not only for your goodness and mercy, but also for your holiness and purity. Make me holy and I shall be happy. From now on, I turn away from the sins I have deliberately set my heart on, and I commit myself to a constant battle against those other sins which cling to me. I hate them and pray against them; I want nothing more to do with any of them.' If you accept the Lord on these terms, then he will be your God.

He is also the all-sufficient God who calls you to surrender all you are and all you have to him. Will you let him be your all in all? There is no human need that he cannot satisfy. He can give you a joy and peace that is quite literally out of this world. How do you respond? Do you still want to cling onto the limited pleasures that this life has to offer? Perhaps you would like to have the best of both worlds: God *and* the world because you cannot bear the thought of having God and nothing else. But the Lord Jesus Christ declares that to become a citizen of God's Kingdom is such a precious thing that you will willingly part with everything that stands in your way. He says it is like a merchant who comes across an extremely rare and valuable pearl - so valuable that he will readily sell everything else he has in order to possess it (Matthew 13:45-46). Is anything more worthwhile than belonging to the all-sufficient God? Come to him now and say, 'Lord, I want nothing else besides you. While others may set their hearts on making money, I shall be content with your favour. I look to you for my happiness and I gladly put my trust in you. If I know you as my God and my salvation I shall be content. I yield myself to you without reservation; I bring no conditions. Everything else I leave to you. Whether you give me more or less of earthly things, anything or nothing, I shall remain satisfied in the assurance that you are my God.' Come to him in this spirit and you will never be disappointed.

This gracious, holy and all-sufficient God is also the sovereign Lord who says to you, 'If you want me to be your God, you must give me the supremacy. You must not make me second to any sin or personal ambition. If you want to belong to me, you must acknowledge me as your Lord and Master. Will you submit to my rule, my Word and my discipline?' How do you respond to this God? Bow before him and confess, 'Lord, I would far rather live to please you than please myself. I would far rather see your will done than my own. I acknowledge your laws to be good and right and count it a privilege to be under them. And although I have a sinful heart which is inclined to break your law, I have made up my mind that I want nobody else to govern my life besides you. I take you as my Lord and I commit myself to worship, obey, love and serve you for the rest of my life.' There is no other fitting way to respond to God's sovereignty.

Again, the Lord tells you, 'I am the true and faithful God. If you want me to be your God, you must be content to trust me. Will you take me at my word and depend on my faithfulness? Will you be content to suffer poverty, affliction and persecution in this life and to wait for heaven to receive your reward? My promises are not always fulfilled instantly; will you have the patience to wait?' Will you have this God as your God? Are you

84

content to live by faith and trust him for an unseen happiness, an unseen heaven and an unseen glory? Does your heart reply, 'Lord, I will trust you. I commit myself to you and I cast myself upon you. I am willing to take you at your word. I would rather have your promises than any of my possessions and I would rather have the sure hope of heaven than all the joys that this earth has to offer.' The Lord will never fail to hear such a cry. When you turn to him, you must acknowledge him to be the God he has shown himself to be. You cannot accept his mercy while you continue to love sin and hate holiness and you cannot receive him as your Benefactor so long as you refuse to submit to him as your Sovereign.

7. Believe in the Lord Jesus Christ

Only Jesus Christ can rescue you from the misery into which your sins have plunged you and he freely offers himself to you. No matter how many sins you have committed, no matter how great they are and no matter how deeply-rooted they have become, you can still be saved. The Lord Jesus calls you to look to him. 'Look to me and be saved, all you ends of the earth!' he declares (Isaiah 45:22). If you come to him, you have his word that he will never turn you away (John 6:37). He pleads with you to be reconciled to God (2 Corinthians 5:20). If you are eternally separated from God, it will be only because you refused to come to him for life (John 5:40). Don't let your sense of unworthiness hold you back. It is not your unworthiness that is the problem so much as your unwillingness. I appeal to you to come to Christ now! Accept him as your Prophet - the final and supreme revelation of God; accept him as your Priest - the one and only mediator between God and man; and accept him as your King - the sovereign Lord of heaven and earth. Of course, you must first of all sit down and count the cost of coming to Christ. You must deny yourself, you must be prepared to suffer for him and

85

you must go wherever he directs. Are you determined to stick with him through thick and thin? If so, you will never perish and you have passed from death to life.

(a) Yield yourself to him

When you truly trust in Jesus Christ, all your faculties are given up to him. You yield everything you are to him in order that he may be glorified both in your body and your spirit. Any prejudices you may have had against him are now firmly in the past; your *judgement* and *understanding* now unite to acknowledge him as worthy of your honour, love and eternal adoration. Your *will* submits to him, 'Lord, your love has overcome me. You have won me and you shall have me.' You yield your *memory* to Christ, 'Lord, here is a storehouse for you. Clear out all the rubbish I have stored here for so long and fill me with your truth, your promises and your ways.' Your *conscience* declares, 'From now on, Lord, I am going to side with you. I will warn when the sinner is tempted and I will smite when you are offended. I will witness for you and judge for you, and guide into your ways, and I will never again allow sin to dwell in peace and quiet in this soul.' Your *feelings* will also belong to Christ - to love him, seek him, fear him and worship him. You will constantly bewail and mourn your own sinfulness and you will be filled with anger and hatred towards everything that dishonours your Saviour.

The Lord Jesus Christ calls for a total commitment to him, 'Whoever of you does not forsake all that he has cannot be my disciple' (Luke 14:33). In comparison with him, you must hate your father, your mother and even your own life (Luke 14:26). In short, you must give him yourself and all that you have without reservation, or else you cannot belong to him.

86

(b) Obey him

If you are going to follow the Lord Jesus Christ, you must make his laws your own and let them govern everything you think, say and do. It is not enough to pick and choose which commandments suit you and which do not; you must obey them all. If you are a true Christian you will have a conscience which is sensitive to little sins and duties as well as those which are greater. You will also be committed to follow Christ when times are hard as much as when things are going more smoothly. The Psalmist wrote, 'I cling to your testimonies... your testimonies I have taken as a heritage for ever... I have inclined my heart to perform your statutes for ever, to the very end... I shall observe your statutes continually' (Psalm 119:31,111,112,117). But having committed yourself to obeying the Lord Jesus, it is important that you go on to do so. The Israelites told Moses that they would do everything God commanded them, but when they faced a time of trial, they demonstrated that they lacked the heart to keep their promise (Deuteronomy 5:27,29).

If you are serious about submitting to Christ's commandments, think about their meaning and their breadth. Remember that they are spiritual; they extend to the very thoughts and inclinations of the heart. If you are going to submit to his law, it will affect your thoughts and your motives. His command-ments are also very strict and demand self-denial. Again, this all runs contrary to your natural inclinations. The Lord Jesus Christ describes becoming a Christian in terms of passing through a narrow gate and following a difficult way (Matthew 7:13-14). Are you determined, in Christ's strength, to perform every duty that you find required of you and to avoid every sin that you find forbidden in God's Word - whether it is something outward or inward? If you are honest you will know that there are some duties which your heart particularly rebels against and

87

there are some sins which pose particular temptations to you. In these areas, above all, you must resolve, by the grace of God, to follow Christ rather than your own sinful inclinations.

8. Seek God's face in prayer

Set apart some time to be alone before God. You will need to earnestly seek his help and to seriously ask yourself whether you are willing to leave your sins and submit yourself to the Lord for the rest of your life. This isn't something you can afford to do casually; there is nothing more important. The Lord has promised to give grace and strength to those who seek him with all their heart. Don't rely on yourself or on your own will-power, but put your trust in God himself.

Take time to prepare yourself to come to the Lord with reverence and humble faith, then bow down before him and pour out your heart in words such as these:

'Holy God, I come trusting in the saving work of your Son and plead with you to accept me. I have turned my back upon you and gone my own way. I am a sinner by nature and by practice and well deserve to be condemned to hell. And yet in your infinite grace, you have promised me mercy if I will only turn to you with all my heart. I have heard the good news of Jesus Christ and I am coming now to submit myself to you. I want to be at peace with you and therefore I am renouncing every idol that I have worshipped in the past and I shall no longer side with any of your enemies. From the bottom of my heart I am committed to fighting against every known sin, making use of every means available to me. I confess with shame that in the past I have set my heart upon the things of this world in an idolatrous manner, but I am here and now yielding my heart to you, the great Creator of all. I look to you, the great and glorious

God, for the grace I shall need to resist all the temptations and attractions of the world so that I shall not turn away from you into the paths of sin. I also ask you to make me victorious over the temptations of the devil. By your grace, I am committed never to give in to his evil suggestions. But because my own righteousness is like filthy rags in your sight, I have no confidence in myself. I depend entirely upon you; in and of myself I am hopeless, helpless and completely powerless to overcome temptation from any source.

'If it were not for your infinite mercy, I would not dare approach you now. But since you have offered, through Christ, to be my God, I am coming to you with awe and confidence. I call upon heaven and earth to witness that from this moment on, you are the Lord my God. I humble myself before your holy majesty and acknowledge you, Father, Son and Holy Spirit, to be my all in all. I yield myself to you, body and soul, to serve you in holiness and righteousness for the rest of my life. And because you have appointed the Lord Jesus Christ as the only way of coming to you, I enter, as it were, into a marriage covenant with him:

'Lord Jesus, I come to you hungry and thirsty, poor and needy, miserable, blind and naked, unclean, unworthy and condemned. I am not worthy to wash the feet of any of your servants let alone be solemnly married to the King of glory. But such is your love that I am here now to take you as my Master and Husband, for better, for worse, for richer, for poorer, in good times and bad times, to love, honour and obey you before anyone else, for ever. I receive you as my Prophet, Priest and King, my Saviour and my Lord. I am unworthy, but you are the Lord my Righteousness. I have no wisdom of my own and I look to you as my only Guide. I commit myself to doing your will and not my own. And since you have told me that if I am to reign with you, I must first of all suffer for you, I am prepared to endure

89

whatever you send my way, looking to you for grace and confident that nothing will ever separate me from you.

'I praise you that you have given me your holy laws to govern and direct me through life and I willingly submit myself to them. All your laws are holy, just and good. From now on, my thoughts, my speech and my actions shall be subject to your Word and even though my sinful heart may continue to rebel, I have no desire to neglect any part of my duty to you. As I come to you, I am very conscious of my own weakness and shortcomings. I am guilty of many unintentional sins and I humbly pray that you will still receive me as you have promised, for my heart is sincerely set upon you.

'Almighty God, Searcher of hearts, I am making this covenant with you today without any conscious hypocrisy or reservations, but if there is any insincerity in my heart, please reveal it to me and put me right.

'God the Father, my God and Father, I praise you for the great plan of salvation you devised for lost and hopeless sinners. God the Son, my Saviour and Redeemer, I praise you for loving me and washing me from my sins in your own blood. God the Holy Spirit, I praise you for turning me from sin to God by your almighty power. High and holy Lord God Almighty, Father, Son and Holy Spirit, I praise you for making me your Friend and, by your infinite grace, for making me your servant. Amen - let it be so. And may the covenant which I have made here on earth be ratified in heaven.'

I encourage you to make a covenant with God, not only in your heart, but in words. You may find it helpful to write it down and then to bring it to him in prayer and to sign it. Then keep it as a reminder and an encouragement when doubts and temptations come.

9. Don't put off turning to God any longer

There is no guarantee that you will have another opportunity to turn to God. If you don't come now, you may find yourself increasingly hardened through the deceitfulness of sin. The day of grace will not continue for ever. Come now! Mercy calls you, the Saviour is waiting to be gracious to you and the Holy Spirit is striving with you. Christ's ministers are calling, conscience is stirring and God is holding out his grace. It is now or never. Be like the Psalmist who said, 'I made haste and did not delay to keep your commandments' (Psalm 119:60). If you reject God's offer of mercy now, he may declare in his wrath that you shall never enter his kingdom. I urge you therefore to do three things and to do them as a matter of urgency:

(a) Make time to hear the Word of God

Every time you read the Bible or listen to its message, remind yourself that this is the Word of God which is living and powerful and is able to save your soul (Hebrews 4:12; James 1:21). Come to it therefore with the express desire, hope and expectation that the Lord will use it to change your heart. When you meet with Christians or hear God's Word preached, think to yourself, 'May today be the day when God shall break into my life!' If you are tempted to think that you have heard the good news of Jesus Christ preached on numerous occasions, but nothing has happened to you so far, let me suggest that you may not have been listening with a spirit of prayerful longing and expectation.

(b) Yield to the work of the Holy Spirit

When the Holy Spirit convicts you of your sins, don't resist him, but rather plead with God to save you and make you his own.

91

And when your conscience is stricken with a sense of your guilt and you are frightened by the thought of eternity, ask God to give you a sure and lasting peace through turning away from all your sins and giving your heart unreservedly to Christ. Say to him, 'Lord, please do not leave the work half-done. Strike at the bottom of my corruption and let out the life-blood of my sins!'

(c) Give yourself to fervent prayer

If you don't pray, there is no evidence that God is at work in you at all. But make sure that you keep on praying. Don't be a hypocrite! Set aside some time every day to pray to God in secret, and if you have a family, call them together and seek God together daily. But if your prayers are cold and lifeless, they won't reach half-way to heaven. You must be earnest and persevering in prayer. Don't be easily put off. Learn to wrestle with God in prayer. Go to him with this kind of spirit, 'Lord, I need your grace and I am determined not to give up seeking you until I have it. I shall keep on pleading with you until you have mercy on me and make me a new person.'

10. Avoid walking into temptation

You will never turn away from sin unless you make an effort to avoid situations where you know you will be tempted to sin. To put yourself in a situation where you know temptation will be lurking is as dangerous as a fish nibbling at the bait or a group of children playing on the edge of a cliff. Some temptations are unavoidable and we can look to God for the grace to help us overcome them, but that is quite a different matter from putting him to the test by running into danger. And one of the most powerful temptations of all is found in the influence of bad company. There have been so many people who have been close to turning to Christ, but then at the last minute they have been pulled back by their friends and placed in a far worse position than they were ever in before. The Bible very plainly states, 'The companion of fools will be destroyed' (Proverbs 13:20). As far as possible, make a clean break from any evil influences. Your life depends upon it!

If God ever changes your heart, other Christians will become your closest friends. Don't add to the obstacles which keep you from trusting Christ by clinging to people who try to mock you out of taking him seriously, or make every effort to prejudice you against a religion which they view as strict, miserable and ridiculous. They may flatter you and appear very persuasive, but remember the warnings the Holy Spirit has given you in the Bible: 'My son, if sinners entice you, do not consent. If they say, "Come with us...Cast in your lot among us"; my son, do not walk in the way with them, keep your foot from their path... Avoid it, do not travel on it; turn away from it and pass on... The way of the wicked is like darkness; they do not know what makes them stumble' (Proverbs 1:10-19; 4:15-19). I am moved when I stop to think of how many people who read these words may be drawn into sin and finally condemned simply because they made no effort to keep away from certain people and places. In the words of Moses to the Israelites, I urge you once again, 'Depart now from the tents of these wicked men!' (Numbers 16:26). Avoid them like the plague!

In seeking the Lord, you may find it helpful to set apart a whole day for prayer and fasting. Examine your heart by reflecting carefully on the Ten Commandments. Write down all the various ways in which you have broken each commandment, both by what you have done and by what you have failed to do. Having made a catalogue of your sins, spread them before the

Lord in shame and sorrow. And then, if you are able to do so, enter into a covenant with him along the lines suggested earlier in this chapter, and may the Lord grant you mercy.

I have now given you ten directions. What will you do with them? Will you now obey the voice of God or will you refuse him? What excuse would you make if, having known the way of life, you were finally condemned because of your stubbornness? Beware of idly neglecting to follow these directions. Wake up - and the Lord will be with you!

THE AWAKENED SINNER THINKS ALOUD

What a miserable person my sins have turned me into! My heart has deceived me for so long into thinking that all was well, when all the time I was lost and condemned. My sins have rendered me unclean and polluted before God - more unpleasant than anything I could possibly imagine. Far from being good, my heart is full of sin. Every part of me is tainted by its deadly poison. I have an aversion towards doing anything good and a proneness to do evil. My heart is the source of an endless flow of sinful thoughts, words and actions. I have broken every single commandment in God's Book and I am left with an infinite debt to him that I can never repay. If the whole world were covered with bank notes and if those notes were stacked so high that they reached heaven, it would still be inadequate to cover my debts to the Bank of heaven. If treason against an earthly monarch is universally regarded as a serious crime, I shudder to think of the enormity of my wickedness in lifting up my hands in defiance against the infinite and all-glorious God.

My sins rise up against me like a multitude of armies. They are as mighty as they are many. Nothing could be so fearsome. My sins are as numerous as the grains of sand on the sea-shore and as mighty as the mountains. It would be better to have rocks and mountains falling upon me than to bear the crushing weight of my own sins. Lord, the weight of my sins is too great for me to bear. Take away my heavy guilt or I shall be crushed without hope and pressed down into hell. You know, O Lord, the full extent of my sinfulness.

How low have my sins brought me! I was created in the image of God; the crown of his creation. Yet here I am, a lump of filthiness, a coffin of rottenness. I am a fallen sinner and my glory has departed. In the eyes of the most holy God, I am more offensive than the most unpleasant of sights could ever be to any man or woman. I am a slave to sin, cast out of God's favour and under God's curse. My sins are unforgiven and I am only a step away from death. What shall I do? Where shall I go? Which way shall I look? The Lord is frowning on me from above, hell is gaping at me from below, my conscience is accusing me on the inside and I face all kinds of dangers and temptations on the outside. Where can I hide from the God who knows everything? And what power can I use to rescue me from the God who is infinite in might?

How can I possibly be content to continue as I am? What is wrong with me? Do I enjoy being miserable? Do I want to go to hell? If I carry on in my sins, I shall definitely be condemned. Am I really so foolish that I am prepared to sell my soul for some fleeting sinful pleasure? Can I really linger in this miserable condition any longer? No! My only hope is to turn from my sins and turn to God through Jesus Christ.

I bow down in worship and adoration before you, O merciful Lord. Without your patience I would already have been condemned for ever. I praise you for your grace and look to you for mercy. I renounce my sins and resolve by your grace to set myself against them and to follow you in holiness and righteousness all the days of my life.

I am not worthy to have anything to do with you at all. Yet you have called me to come to you and so I gladly and thankfully draw near to you. You are mine and I am yours. You are my King and my God; my heart shall be your throne and every faculty that I possess shall come and worship before you. If only my heart were in any way fit for you! I am eternally unworthy to belong to you. But since you call for my heart, I freely give it to you. I wish it were better, but I entrust it into the hands of the only One who can make it new. Mould it after your own heart; make it holy, humble, sensitive to your will and write your law upon it.

Come, Lord Jesus, come quickly. Take hold of my heart in your triumphant power and make me your own for ever. I come to you as the only way to the Father, the only Mediator. By myself I can do nothing; I look to you alone. Save me or else I will surely perish. The wages of sin is death and no one ever deserved its wages more than I do. I deserve to be condemned for ever, but my trust is in you. Your perfect sacrifice on the cross is sufficient to cover all my sins. I submit myself entirely to your authority.

Holy Spirit, the One who strengthens your people and makes them holy, fill me with your fruit of love, joy, peace, patience, kindness, goodness, faithfulness, gentleness and self-control. I yield my body and soul to you to be your dwelling-place. Make me more like the Lord Jesus and use me in your service. For too long I have served the world and heeded Satan's voice, but from now on I want to be governed by you and to live according to your Word.

God the Father, Son and Holy Spirit - One God in Three Persons, I surrender myself to you. Write your name upon me and upon everything I possess; I am no longer my own, but I belong to you. I have chosen to go your way, and even though I cannot perfectly keep even one of your commandments, I shall not allow myself to be complacent about any sin. Give me all the grace I need in order to remain close to you whatever the cost. I am fully convinced that I shall never regret turning to you and I am therefore content to deny myself and suffer for your sake. The happiness and joy I shall experience in heaven will far outweigh any difficulties and trials I may face as a follower of the Lord Jesus here on earth. Let me be poor, insignificant and despised here, so long as I may live and reign with you for ever. Lord, let me never go back on my covenant with you. By your grace, I will live and die for you. This is my everlasting choice. Receive me, I pray. Amen.

7.
Amazing Grace!

I hope I have said enough already about your need to turn to Christ and your desperate condition without him to stir you to action. However, knowing the stubbornness of the human heart, in this chapter I shall focus specifically on the grace and kindness of God to further persuade you to be reconciled to him.

Gracious God, if anyone has managed to read this far without being touched by your Spirit, begin your work in him now. Humble him and make him acknowledge that you are infinitely greater than he is. Am I like a fisherman who has laboured long and hard but all in vain? Lord Jesus, as I come now to cast out my net one last time, stand upon the shore and show me how and where I should spread my net. Give me all the strength and wisdom I need to lead anyone who reads these pages to you and make my net full.

Heaven and earth call you to turn to Christ. Even hell itself urges you to repent. All true Christian ministers labour for you and the heavenly angels are waiting to rejoice over you. Why, then, should the devil laugh at your condemnation? And yet if you do not turn back to God that is precisely what will happen. Would you not rather be a joy to angels than a laughing-stock for demons? In fact, not only would the angels rejoice at your repentance, but God himself would rejoice over you too. The Bible says that 'as the bridegroom rejoices over the bride, so shall your God rejoice over you' (Isaiah 62:5). In the Parable of the Prodigal Son, the Lord Jesus described God's joy over repentant sinners in terms of a father welcoming back his wayward son. You can just picture the father in that story laying aside his dignity and forgetting his age as he runs to embrace his son. His heart is moved and he is full of compassion. He sees him a long way off and rushes to greet him. He says nothing about his ingratitude and rebellion, but receives him with open arms, embraces him and treats him as a guest of honour. He cannot keep his joy to himself but invites others to share it with him: 'for this my son was dead and is alive again; he was lost and is found' (Luke 15:11-32). Such is the love of God to sinful people: his mercy sees us in the distance, his love runs to meet us and usher us home, and his joy overflows and fills the whole of heaven.

Only a rock could fail to be moved by such grace. Are you still holding back? Still resisting God? Still refusing to turn to him? Do you realise that even those who have died without Christ are crying out to you from their place of torment, urging you to repent? The Lord Jesus spoke of one such man who pleaded with heaven to send someone to the members of his family who were still alive in order that they might be saved. Surely, he thought to himself, if someone goes to them from the dead, they are bound to repent (Luke 16:27-30). Think for a moment about the horrors of hell: the bottomless pit, the chains of darkness, the gnawing worm, the raging fire, the endlessly rising smoke. Is that where you are going? Can you hear the curses and blasphemies, the weepings and wailings, the roaring and groaning and gnashing of teeth? How terrible it would be if God were to open the mouth of hell so that we could hear the miserable and eternal cries of the lost. If you do not turn to Christ, all this is only a matter of hours away.

If there is any wisdom in the world, surely it is to come to Christ. If there is anything that is right, anything that is reasonable, this is it. And if there is anything foolish, unreasonable and absurd, it is to remain as you are. I urge you, then, to sit down and consider these five further points and to ask yourself whether it is not the most reasonable thing in the world for you to repent and turn to the Saviour.

You should turn to him because:

1. The God who made you graciously invites you

God is so kind, compassionate and merciful that he calls you to come to him. As the heavens are higher than the earth, so are his ways above our ways and his thoughts above our thoughts. He is 'full of compassion, and gracious, longsuffering and abundant in mercy' (Psalm 86:15). The Bible therefore appeals to you to 'Return to the Lord your God, for he is gracious and merciful, slow to anger and of great kindness; and he relents from doing harm' (Joel 2:13). What greater encouragement do you need? If there were no hope of mercy, then I could understand you holding back. But there has never been any earthly ruler as kind and patient as the Lord. In wonder and adoration, Micah declared, 'Who is a God like you, pardoning iniquity?' (Micah 7:18). This is the God you have to deal with! He delights in mercy. If you will simply turn to him, he will have compassion on you; he will subdue your iniquities and cast all your sins into the depths of the sea (Micah 7:19). '"Return to me, and I will return to you," says the Lord of hosts' (Malachi 3:7). While it is all too easy to overlook God's justice or to presume on God's mercy apart from Christ, you can never overestimate his kindness and love. God's mercy exceeds our imagination. The Bible describes God's mercies as great, manifold, tender, sure and everlasting. And they are all yours, if you will only turn to him. Are you willing to come? A throne of grace awaits you; the king himself invites you. He is the God who keeps 'mercy for thousands, forgiving iniquity and transgression and sin' (Exodus 34:7). Reflecting on the Lord's dealings with his people, one of Israel's greatest leaders worshipped him and said, 'But you are God, ready to pardon, gracious and merciful, slow to anger, abundant in kindness' (Nehemiah 9:17).

God's invitation to you is earnest, loving and persistent. "'Return...," says the Lord, "And I will not cause my anger to fall on you; for I am merciful," says the Lord, "And I will not remain angry for ever. Only acknowledge your iniquity, that you have transgressed against the Lord your God"' (Jeremiah 3:12-13). "'As I live," says the Lord God, "I have no pleasure in the death of the wicked, but that the wicked turn from his way and live. Turn, turn from your evil ways! For why should you die...?"' (Ezekiel 33:11). "'If a wicked man turns from all his sins which he has committed, keeps all my statutes and does what is lawful and right, he shall surely live; he shall not die. None of the transgressions which he has committed shall be remembered against him; because of the righteousness which he has done, he shall live... Repent, and turn from all your transgressions, so that iniquity will not be your ruin. Cast away from you all the transgressions which you have committed, and get yourselves a new heart and a new spirit. For why should you die...? For I have no pleasure in the death of one who dies," says the Lord God. "Therefore turn and live!"' (Ezekiel 18:21-22, 30-32).

These are not man's words, but God's words - the holy and righteous God who has been offended, insulted and blasphemed. Yet, in his infinite mercy he has not given up on you. He seeks you and pleads for you. Doesn't it move you and break your heart?

2. The doors of heaven are thrown open to you

The Lord Jesus Christ calls you to become a citizen of the kingdom of heaven. There is no kingdom on earth half so vast or so glorious. We cannot begin to imagine what it will be like when the full glory of God's kingdom is revealed. The Bible describes it in terms of a city of pure gold with foundations adorned by precious stones and gates of pearl. It will be illuminated by glory and God himself will be its temple. All this, and more, the Lord tells you he will give you if you will bow down and worship him, receive his mercy and submit to his Son. How foolish and hard-hearted you must be if you would rather serve the world and neglect eternal glory!

Think for a moment about what is being offered to you: a blessed kingdom, a kingdom of glory, a kingdom of righteousness, a kingdom of peace, an everlasting kingdom. And here you shall live and reign for ever. The Lord himself will seat you on a throne of glory and place the royal diadem upon your head. The crown that he shall give you will not be one of thorns, for there will be no sin or suffering there, but a crown of life, a crown of righteousness, a crown of glory. Your body, created out of the dust of the earth, will shine brighter than the stars. If you say you believe what the Bible reveals about heaven, what are you going to do about it? Will you give up your sins and your self-seeking? Are you prepared to deny yourself and follow the Lord, putting to death all your sinful inclinations and desires? If you are, then the kingdom is yours - for ever.

I am sure you will agree that the offer is a fair one. It is right and proper for God to punish and condemn those who refuse his invitation. But make sure that you are not among them. Take the Lord at his word. Let go of this world and take hold of eternal life and happiness!

3. God will change your life for the better now

Not all of God's blessings are in the future. When you turn to Christ, you are redeemed from slavery to sin, you are released from bondage to the spirit of the present age and you are set free from the grip of the devil. You need no longer live in fear of death and judgement and you can face any trials and sufferings which the Lord sends your way with confidence and assurance that nothing will separate you from his love.

The Lord himself will be a Friend and a Father to you. He will be both a Sun and a Shield to you. In a word he will be God to you. And what more can be said? He will do for you and be to you everything you would expect God to do and be. He will give you grace and glory and will withhold nothing good from you. He will adopt you as his sons and daughters and make you heirs of his promises. He will establish his everlasting covenant with you and no one will be able to make a valid accusation against you - not the law, not your conscience, not even the devil; God has declared you perfectly righteous and acceptable to him through Jesus Christ. The Lord will give you free access into his presence and he will answer your prayers. You will enjoy communion and fellowship with him and he will order everything that happens to you for your good.

4. God has done everything that needs to be done

The Lord has stooped as low as he possibly can without staining the glory of his holiness. None of us could ever have atoned for our own sins and it is beyond our power to fully obey God's law. But God does not make unreasonable or impossible demands upon us. He has sent his own dear Son, the Lord Jesus Christ, to live and die in our place. All we are required to do is believe in him - the atoning Saviour and our perfect Righteousness.

There are many people who would prefer to engage in some rigorous and demanding exercise in order to be saved. They would willingly go to live in the desert or suffer hunger and thirst if that is what God required. But the Lord requires nothing of the sort. There is nothing we can do to 'earn' our salvation, nothing we can contribute. The Lord Jesus has done it all. But perhaps you are thinking, 'I can see the truth in what you are saying, but I just can't bring myself to repent and believe. I just can't do it!' Let me offer you some final words of encouragement by saying to you:

5. God will even give you the grace you need to turn to him

The Lord Jesus Christ reaches out his hand to raise you out of your sins and into his Kingdom. You have no excuse. If you are condemned, it will be because you have refused his help. He will give you sight for your blindness, a covering for your nakedness and riches for your poverty. He offers you his own righteousness and grace to bring you to God. But you may object, 'I have nothing to offer him in return.' You don't need to! God's grace is free. All you have to do is to seek him with all your heart and beg for his mercy. The Lord commands you to know and fear him. Perhaps again you reply, 'Yes, but my mind is blinded and my heart is hard; I can't bring myself to know him and fear him.' You are quite correct, but God offers to enlighten your mind and teach you to fear him. The Bible says, 'Yes, if you cry out for discernment and lift up your voice for understanding, if you seek her as silver and search for her as for hidden treasures; then you will understand the fear of the Lord and find the knowledge of God. For the Lord gives wisdom; from his mouth come knowledge and understanding' (Proverbs 2:3-6). Although you cannot do anything by yourself, the Holy Spirit offers to give you the strength you need. You can't change your heart any more than a leopard can wash away its spots, but the Lord can make you clean. Surrender yourself to him and ask him to do for you and in you what you can never do for yourself.

8.
Wake up and Live!

In the previous chapters I have attempted to impress upon you your desperate need of the Lord Jesus Christ. I must now ask you what you intend to do. Are you going to stay as you are and go to hell or are you going to turn to him and receive eternal life? How much longer will you remain undecided? You have a simple choice to make: a choice between eternal bliss and eternal torment, between the polluted pool of sin or the pure water of life which is freely available from the throne of God. It is foolish to invest all your time and energy in this world because you can't take anything with you when you die. Only Christ can give you a joy, a peace and an inheritance that lasts for ever. You must commit yourself wholeheartedly and unreservedly to him. Don't be content to be like King Agrippa in the Bible, who was 'almost persuaded' but did nothing about it (Acts 26:28). If you sit on the fence and refuse to commit yourself, you will be condemned along with all the outright unbelievers.

I urge you not to put off your response until later because if you won't turn back to God now while you are conscious of his gracious invitations, you are far less likely to do so later when any impression he has made upon you has worn off and your heart is further hardened through sin. Submit yourself to Jesus Christ now. The Bible says, 'Now is the accepted time; behold, now is the day of salvation' (2 Corinthians 6:2). Today could be the very day from which you date your eternal happiness.

Why remain in your dangerous and terrible condition one day longer? What if the Lord should require your soul tonight? Many have allowed their day of opportunity to pass by and have gone to their doom. I pray that you will find peace with God before it is too late.

If the choice you have to make is as stark as I have said it is - between life and death, what keeps you from choosing life? The only thing that could possibly be holding you back is your own stubborn will. Turn away from your sins, deny yourself and trust in Christ, and he will be yours. Shake off your complacency and indifference and lay aside all your excuses. You know all too well that the Lord is better than sin. Why, then, do you insist on resisting him and clinging to your sins?

As you have been reading, have you felt your heart warmed by the Word of God? Have you found yourself almost persuaded to leave your sins and turn to Christ? It may well be that the Holy Spirit has been speaking to you without your being conscious of it. But the Holy Spirit will not strive with you for ever. Again I urge you to turn now, while God is giving you the time and opportunity to do so. The Lord Jesus himself calls you to come to him. His arms are outstretched to receive you. His words are full of grace and kindness: 'If anyone thirsts, let him come to me and drink' (John 7:37). 'Come to me, all you who labour and are heavy laden, and I will give you rest. Take my yoke upon you and learn from me, for I am gentle and lowly in heart, and you will find rest for your souls' (Matthew 11:28-29). 'The one who comes to me, I will by no means cast out' (John 6:37). Throw yourself into the arms of his love!

The Lord Jesus has thrown wide open the doors of your prison. You need not be held in the chains of your sins any longer. He calls you to come out - to be free to serve him. Are you going to just sit there when in the service of God you will find freedom, peace and joy?

As I conclude, I am fearful that when you put this book down, you may be no different from when you first picked it up. You may have stayed with me all the way through and still not abandoned your sins and put your trust in the Lord Jesus Christ. Have I been wasting my time? As far as you are concerned, perhaps I have. But to ignore my words is one thing; to ignore the words of God is another. And if you reject the gracious invitations of the Lord Jesus Christ and resist the Holy Spirit by refusing to repent of your sins, you are dishonouring the God who made you.

Let me issue one final plea to you to wake up and live. I wish I could stand on some high place and cry out like Jeremiah, 'O earth, earth, earth, hear the word of the Lord!' (Jeremiah 22:29). Unless you have already made up your mind to die as you are, listen once more to the voice of mercy:

> Ho! Everyone who thirsts, come to the waters;
> And you who have no money, come, buy and eat.
> Yes, come, buy wine and milk without money and
>   without price.
> Why do you spend money for what is not bread,
> And your wages for what does not satisfy?
> Listen diligently to me, and eat what is good,
> And let your soul delight itself in abundance.
> Incline your ear, and come to me,
> Hear, and your soul shall live;
> And I will make an everlasting covenant with you
>   (Isaiah 55:1-3).

The invitation is extended to all. Whether your besetting sin is one of pride, anger, lust or greed, come to the heavenly Physician. He is the one who can heal all kinds of diseases. He will relieve you of your distress. When you are joined to him, you are saved from the wrath of God; you need never again be afraid of God's law. Come to Christ and he will give you spiritual light and understanding. Humble yourself before God and he will teach you his way. Return to the Lord and he will have mercy on you. You may have blasphemed him, cursed him and insulted him; you may have worshipped and served other gods, but if you turn to the Saviour, 'though your sins are like scarlet, they shall be as white as snow; and though they are red like crimson, they shall be as wool' (Isaiah 1:18).

Pleasure-seekers - take to heart God's words of wisdom! 'Forsake foolishness and live, and go in the way of understanding' (Proverbs 9:6).

Mockers - hear the word of the Lord! Even though you have ridiculed Christians for what they believe and the way they live, and even though you have laughed at Christ himself, still the Lord Jesus calls you to himself. Come to him and you will be washed, sanctified and justified in the name of the Lord Jesus and by the Spirit of our God (1 Corinthians 6:11).

Professing Christians - make sure you are *real* Christians! Don't be content with an outward show of religion, but repent and turn to Christ.

Whoever you are and whatever you have done, mercy has been offered to you. 'I call heaven and earth as witnesses today against you, that I have set before you life and death, blessing and cursing; therefore choose life, that...you may live' (Deuteronomy 30:19). I can do no more than warn you and reason with you. I cannot force you to be happy - if I could, I would. What, then, will you do? How do you respond to the Word of God? If you have heard God's call of mercy and refused it, your condemnation on the Day of Judgement will be even greater than that of those who never heard. Is that what you want?

If you have any concern about where you will spend eternity, receive God's mercy now. If you recognise the authority of the God who made you, obey him and come to Christ. If you want to receive God's grace and don't want to close the door of God's mercy upon yourself, then repent. Don't let heaven's doors stand open for you in vain. Don't let the gracious invitations of the Lord Jesus Christ to you be in vain. Don't let the Holy Spirit and his servants strive with you in vain.

Father in heaven, I do not have the power to melt hard hearts, but nothing is impossible with you. Continue your work although I have finished mine. Just one word from your lips is enough. Open this hard heart and let the King of Glory enter in. Do not allow the devil to harden him further against you and keep him from putting off what needs to be done. Give him the will and the power to turn away from his sins and receive eternal life on your terms. Lord God, do not allow the time I have spent in writing these words be for nothing. Put your hand on the heart of this reader and send your Spirit to do his sovereign work. And on the last day, may there be many who will testify that they were brought to you through the words of this book. Amen.